# BIBLIODEATH
# MY ARCHIVES
## WITH LIFE IN FOOTNOTES

### ANDREI CODRESCU

ANTIBOOKCLUB

Cover detail from Albrecht Dürer's *Apocalypse*,
showing St. John devouring the Book (1498)

Library of Congress Control Number: 2012944956

ISBN 978-0-9838683-3-0

Cover design by Gabriel Levinson & Will Petty
Book design by Will Petty

Published in the United States by ANTIBOOKCLUB

www.ANTIBOOKCLUB.com

10 9 8 7 6 1 2 3 4 5

FIRST EDITION

# THANKS

*to Elaine Smyth,*
*who suggested to the editors of a book about the private libraries of authors*
*that they ask me to write a brief essay about my experience with Archives.*
*Most of my books and papers in English are in the keeping of LSU's Hill Memorial,*
*while my Romanian-language materials rest with the Slavic Library at the*
*University of Illinois, Urbana-Champaign. As soon as I set to the task, I realized*
*that I was holding the philosopher's walking stick in my hand, and "brief" is*
*not what happened. Elaine read the first draft of what became a book and*
*encouraged me with helpful suggestions.*

*I am grateful also to J.J. Phillips,*
*former archivist at Berkeley's Bancroft Library,*
*who provided a visceral key to one of my main concerns.*

# BIBLIODEATH

is a transparent death. It is also a public death, an execution witnessed by hundreds of millions of people, the whole literate world, who, with exceptions, is enjoying the spectacle. The public execution of the paper book today is not an attempt to erase the content, like book burnings by the Inquisition or by nazis; it is in fact the opposite: it is the transfer of the content to a new life in another medium. The literate millions watching the guillotine are privy to the first public demonstration of the passage of the soul from one body into another, a reincarnation that is not a metaphysics. Yet for all that, the soul does (not) move to a better place, where it may be cleansed or overlinked, though it is surely lightened. The former body of the book also preserves the original content, making it still useful to the old reading habit.

In the Place de la Rèpublique, where the bibliodeath orgy unfolds, there are exceptions to the merriment, people who are neither singing nor knitting nor holding up their screen to capture the souls of departing books. Many of these exceptionals are liberal humanists shaped in the 20th century by the books whose souls are migrating into screens. These are reasonable and educated people who see a dark logic in their feeling of doom, but cannot articulate it in the language the orgiasts emit. The other exceptionals are the crazies. They cannot articulate a beautiful liberal humanist sentence if their life depended on it, but while they can sing and howl as good as the rest, their bodies are heavy with foreboding and full of dark water. This is a water that reaches them through crazy channels from two vast oceans that lie just outside the island of the bibliodeath orgy, two oceans that the majority of the celebrants know little about. These two oceans, whose powerful waves are battering the shores of 21st-century's auto-da-fé and sending streams through the crazies' channels, are the Archives Ocean and the Sacred Ocean. Both are vast.

The Archives Ocean covers some ten to fifteen thousand years of human expression, fifty-five hundred of which are the written language and five hundred of which are the age of the printed book. The Archives Ocean is widest in the area of the printed books' half-millennium, and deepest in the five thousand years of writing. What lies beyond is fragmentary, a terra incognita of bones and cave art. The bibliodeath orgy concerns only the Archives Ocean half-millennium, but the disturbance runs through the immensity of all its waters.

The Sacred Ocean covers the entirety of human consciousness. It is bigger than the Archives Ocean by the unknown amount of time it took humans to translate awe into gesture. Before expression there were other waters that had seen the void, the birth of matter, the clouds of floating theories. The Sacred Ocean is where the majority of people on earth live and fish for their daily subsistence. They worship the Sacred Ocean, particularly that part which covers their sacred writings, whether in manuscript or book form. The strength of their belief seems like a mere complication to the partiers on the bibliodeath island, but if these technodrunks would put down their photocameras for a minute and sit quiet, they would instantly hear those voices. As it is, they do hear them through the media, but I doubt if they understand them.[1] The desecrated sacred book can only be a *book*. Holy texts, among them the Quran and the Bible, exist in every format but there are no riots over the removal of such a text from an electronic library, and there never will be. One can insult a book on the internet and cause a reality-based riot, but no such demonstration is possible if an individual or even an organization removes a sacred text from its devices. A mob crazed by a virtual relic is hard to imagine, but a book, sacred or not, is in fact a virtuality that has somehow, at some time, become a relic. A virtual reliquary drains belief from the believer if herm[2] realizes that it is virtual; it is a true miracle of the Catholic Church that it has continued to exist by investing the symbolic sacraments with the power of the original. This miracle was doubtlessly

[1] To give but two examples: in February 2012 "[a] fourth day of protests in Afghanistan has left at least twelve more people dead and forced the closure of a foreign military base, as Afghans express their anger at the burning of Qurans at a US air field." (*Global Post*) and October 2010: "Muslims in southern Malawi have been burning Bibles to protest their distribution in Islamic schools by Gideon's International, a Muslim Association of Malawi official said yesterday. The Bibles 'annoyed some parents and other leaders, who have resorted to burning the holy books . . . in protest,' said Sheik Imran Sharif." (*intangiblesoul.wordpress.com*)

[2] "Herm" is my term, standing tersely, I hope, for that ungainly "he/she" or the even clunkier "him or her" or vice-versa. Launched in my book, *whatever gets you through the night: a story of sheherezade and the arabian entertainments* (Princeton University Press, 2011), it explains there its raison d'être better than I can now. Do note, however, that I know a "herm" means also a Greek pedestal: that meaning is intended as well, in the sense that anyone encompassing both genders is, to a certain extent, "petrified."

accomplished by keeping the number of sacraments to two—bread and wine, body and blood—and equating the symbolic rhetoric of transference with the mystery of transubstantiation itself. Such feat of rhetoric took a millennium to accomplish. Our time, and current ocean weather, won't allow for such luxury of time. The fury of believers at the desecration of holy books was matched over time by the fury directed by the clergy at books that questioned the holy books. The generalized anger roiling this area of the Sacred Ocean has to do with the impossibility of containing all the vast workings of the Sacred Ocean into a single wave, or a single book. This profound unsettling is at the core of another powerful opposition: to the knowledge that the Archives Ocean is indifferent to the motions of the Sacred Ocean. The Archives Ocean is turbulent where it meets the Sacred Ocean around the island of the bibliodeath orgy, but it mostly goes about the job of gathering to itself all that can be known and traced about the humans who form both bodies of water. The Sacred Ocean would like to overcome the Archives Ocean, but the orgiastic island now stands between them.

The above are not mere metaphors. The technology that allows for the infinite reproduction of books and for archiving all that is known and can be digitized has unsettled both the world of Archives and the unarchivable but profound worship of the written word. The techno-driven bibliodeath party on the island of the Place de la Rèpublique, which separates the two oceans, is the celebration of an undeniable triumph. Technology has liberated the word both from the coffin of the book and from the limitations of memory. It has won.

But what has it defeated? By incorporating, like the Roman Empire, the painted savages of mumbo-jumbo, it can only improve lives and insure the survival of humans by growing their brains to care for the universe. Right? But the question persists: what has technology defeated? Without falling into the romantic claptrap of the virtues of painted savages who, we now know, were rarely kind to one another, there is still something that the machine has conquered. What is it? I have no idea, which is what this book is groping toward: an idea of homo scribus who lost the war with techne. It happened to me in my lifetime.

This is the story of a writer fast-tracked by the zeitgeist from the awakening of his mind in calligraphy to its maturity through a half-century of quickly morphing technologies of keyboards and memory. It is intended to be a thriller. The suspense rests on the question of what is it that invents and communicates regardless of its (definitely) mortal coil, and who done it, is still doing it, and why. There are also suggestions for creative uses of the guillotined objects. The writer and detective are not one. Take, for example, Raymond Queneau's Morcol in *Le vol d'Icare*: one is an investigator hired by passeist writers to elucidate the mystery of the disappearance of their characters (who fled their conventional romantic fates for modern Paris), the other is Morcol, the private man who, despite being hired, helps the characters escape. This second Morcol is a critic who dooms a century's literature by betraying his employers, who have their own doubts. Queneau finds it amusing. Is it a bloody revolution, an evolution, or are characters just whores? The writers want to know. The answers are various but Morcol will have to, nonetheless, get paid.

The second major protagonist in my story is an elegist who believes that his life and writing are one, and is seriously trying to download his living body alongside his writing into the current technology, which is incapable of it (yet). Hence, a sort of histrionic humanism and an attempt to find the next machine through poetic math. The resort to alchemy has as much chance of success as Giordano Bruno's similar foolishness, but giving up meant not writing the book at all, an impossible nonactivity for a lifelong pollinator.

To the extent that a utopic bildungsroman essaying a major human change can contain ideas bigger than its author, I've also taken a few dives into the above-mentioned oceans, with particular attention to the Archives Ocean, which is the most endangered of the two bodies of the water surrounding the festival of bibliodeath.

# ARCHIVALLY SPEAKING,

there are three types of authors, and I've been all three of them: the Preserver, the Piler, and the Carpe Diem. When I first started writing at fourteen, I had a lined notebook that separated each line of poetry from another, allowing for space between the lines, slow penmanship, eraser-and-end-of-pencil chewing, and the lost gaze looking through and beyond the notebook to the goddess of Inspiration who hovered (now near, now far) like a tree deleafing itself in autumn. I decided to call this state of hypnagogic laziness "poetic contemplation," and woe unto the interrupter—aka mother, teachers, and all classmates except for a couple of girls who were somehow part of the shape of Inspiration itself, a dense, female-shaped fog that awakened lines of poetry in my breast. ("Lines" is the operating word here, because the sense of order I found in the notebook and in the words that aligned themselves lyrically was a splendid excuse for adolescence.) My first poems, having done their measured apprenticeship, were well received, and I started thinking of them as objects of some value, pressed within the pages of the notebook like banknotes. As my reading expanded, I discovered that the more modern poets varied their lines in ways that the lined notebook did not accommodate unless I wrote over the lines or across or under them, a rebellion I was not yet ready to undertake. Reading critical essays about poetry in the Romanian literary weeklies, which were generous to young poets, I also discovered that true poets kept notes of their thoughts, which later could turn into poems. The form of the journal itself was highly prized, but I got the idea fairly early that the diary, or the factual journal, was a prose writer's shop. I had no intention of recalling the details of my life, which were uninteresting to me: what passed for reality was painful and boring, like adults, who were the cumulative sum of all that boredom. Adults were, in effect, complete diaries of all the dull things that went on day after day. They were prose. Poetry—especially in its unlined, free range—was of another order, as were the thinking notes it required. So I acquired a very rare, very expensive, unlined cardboard-bound notebook from Kniga Russkaya, the Russian bookstore that was not frequented by any self-respecting citizen of my town; it was a severe, cold room lined with the red-bound, gold-lettered spines of the classics of communism. The shop broadcast loud Soviet music and was manned by two severe Russian women sent to our town by the KGB to educate us. But they did have stationary. After making sure nobody saw me, I opened the door and slipped in to find my notebook. I paid for it, checked the deserted street again for possible acquaintances, and re-emerged into the sunlight a modern poet with an unlined notebook. The door snapped behind me like the bolt of a rifle.

All religions have murky beginnings and a huge flaw in their founding, which is why they eventually become great, if they do: they expand considerable effort to correct the ontological flaw. Likewise, as soon as I was in possession of my communist-bookstore-originating-unlined notebook, I proceeded to write in it thoughts and verses that were filled with religiosity, decadence, disobedience and profanity—things that defied the ethos of communism as we were taught it. Of course, growing up in the well-behaved medieval citadel of Sibiu founded by orderly Saxons, I had little idea of what those things were. "Religious" meant sneaking into empty churches and breathing in deeply their je ne sais quoi of dust, history, incense, and then listening with ecstatic tremor to the bells that rang the warnings of time to no one in particular. (The people in town, including my mother, obeyed the time of factory whistles and school chimes. The churches had long ceased to function as either reminders to prayer or memento mori; the bell-ringers were volunteers, old men who hadn't died in the war and expressed their gratitude by pulling on the ropes.) As for "decadence" it was a word, but it was a word that defined the idea of modern "poet," who was maudit like Baudelaire, sexually deviant like Rimbaud, alcoholic like Bacovia, and a womanizer like Nichita Stănescu—names that just about covered the pantheon of allowed reading in 1960. My own access to "decadence" was limited to a wet, half-smoked cigarette dangling from my lower lip and a myopic stare of contempt at anything that smacked of the approved order. "Profanity" was, of course, easily available and not far from anyone's lips or mind. The favorite Romanian curse had a short and long form; the short, *Dute-n măta!*[3], was common, like a sneeze, but the long, *Dute-n*

---

[3] *Get back into your mother!*

*pizda măti!*[4], could be a fighting matter. Both long and short meant the same thing: *You're so stupid you should go get born again, maybe you'll get it right if you start over.* The ubiquity of this curse was directed both outward at society in general, and inward at the individual muttering it. Outwardly, it was sincere amazement that a clever people had been duped en masse (or forced) to participate in an ideology that made life miserable; inwardly it was self-reproach at one's cowardly inability to do anything about it. Even addressed to another person, this curse had a social dimension, a plea of "leave me alone," which was nearly impossible in a city with ears in the walls, and citizens required to participate in mass manifestations of official optimism about a future that everyone, including the overseers, didn't believe in. My notebook—soon full of religion, decadence and profanity—contained these violations chaotically, not in any sensical order. To emanate religious sentiments was to align myself with the traditional mystical poets of the pre-war era: Lucian Blaga and Ion Barbu, to name two, who had been right-wing ideologues using mysticism to reinforce their theories. I didn't know anything about this aspect of their interests, but I was genuinely moved and chilled to my depths by their verses; they hinted at the possibility of existence outside the body, and the presence of a universal Panic god that made all things both material and immaterial. Being Jewish, I steered instinctively away from Christian orthodoxy and its hypnotic christic repetitions; I didn't care for Jesus until I found out that he was a Jew, but that was much later, in my twenties, when I was already an American. As for "decadence," I saw it as a reinforcer of mysticism, rather than blasphemy, a reaching out for godlike powers of creation

[4] *Get back into your mother's cunt!*

through a rimbaudlian "derangement of the senses." I got drunk with my literary-inclined gang (mostly just three of us) in a lowlife tavern called The Golden Barrel, where we displayed defiance by reciting out loud poetry, both bawdy and philosophically inaccessible, to the smelly crowd of bitter alcoholics in their oil-stained work overalls. We were "bohemians," and we weren't putting up with it. Now and then one of the annoyed workers would advise us to get born again in the long form, but we laughed it off; they would have whopped our asses otherwise, anyway. My notebook filled steadily with thoughts of the requirements of poetry, opinions about my readings, savage critiques of the provincial poets in my town, and verses redolent of cheap wine and boy hormones. The notebook was always by my elbow, my pencil always at the ready, and I probably wrote more than I drank, abstracting myself from the general hilarity or despondency by giving form to my thoughts. This notebook became everything to me: it was the archive of my young mind taking to a path that would lead, I well knew, sigh, to relentless suffering and ignominious death, as Wordsworth had warned but which I conceived of at the time as the only possible modus vivendi in a society as repressive, repressed, provincial (and boring) as ours. I took three years, from 1960 to 1963, to nearly fill my notebook, which turned out to be as capacious as the Soviet Union where it came from.[5]

[5] **A Chekhov Novella**: The Writers' Workshop, Sibiu branch, provided much of its content as my poetic education grew by leaps and bounds. The Sibiu Writers' Workshop, open to the public, met every Wednesday in an unheated room on the second floor of a mighty 17th-century building that housed all-important administrative offices, including our House of Culture. Seated on hard straight-backed wooden chairs, ten to fifteen attendees represented all of Sibiu: a shy proletarian who'd written a poem after hearing an afterwork literature lecture, a jeweler from the town's medieval center who also collected books, two retired teachers (one of whom was a licensed hunter, and the other a bookish old maid who wept at the slightest hint of sentiment), a strong young fop who wore a leather jacket, a portly doctor, an ancient reputed to be a "philosopher," several high school girls, and one boy (me). We lived in different parts of the city; Sibiu retained, remarkably late in the 20th century, the medieval layout of the guilds: the old center city, dating from the 11th through the 16th centuries, had seen witch burnings, impalements by Vlad Dracul, demonstrations, executions, and a Viennese orchestra performing the waltzes of Richard Strauss; the old, crooked houses had oblong windows in the pitched roofs, the "eyes of Sibiu," eyes that followed you everywhere, but which had seen everything from marching armies to guilty husbands returning home at

dawn (my father). A medieval bridge called "The Liars' Bridge" connected the hilltop center with the concentrically more modest (and newer) neighborhoods outside the walls of the original fortified city. The old town was home to printers, watchmakers, repairmen, jewelers and photographers (my mother and father). In the old city center stood also the palaces of power: our own building, formerly the home of Transylvanian governor Baron von Bruckenthal, now the headquarters of the Romanian Communist Party's regional institutions; the Bruckenthal Museum across the square, built for the governor's art collection; the 12th-century Catholic cathedral with its 15th-century clock tower; the Town Hall; the Imparatul Romanilor Hotel (Emperor of the Romans) where my father had wasted his youth "on women and cards" (my mother's words); and the two Austro-Hungarian-era restaurants that still served spicy paprikash when they found beef (otherwise, the stiff-jacketed waiters solemnly brought out chicken noodle soup in porcelain toureens and poured it with silver ladles into the bowls of Party officials and their guests or young mistresses). Here also stood a sturdy stone cube, a defiant remnant of the dead German empire, which was also my prison, the Gheorghe Lazar Lyceum, my high school. In the Center one heard German, Hungarian, and Romanian, in that order, and on Sundays the smell of fresh apple strudel wafted from every doorway. I don't remember how I first got to the Writers' Workshop, around age fourteen, but I quickly learned that my first timid attempts at lyric were more interesting and more melodic than the jeweler's, who lived in the butler's closet in a once-grand apartment divided by the authorities into twelve living spaces with a communal kitchen, or the straight-out-of-Chekhov doctor who dabbed with a checkered cloth inelegantly and often at his sweaty forehead, and certainly hardier than those of the poetesses' who threw her head back, closed her eyes, and transpired slightly when she recited her love lyrics to a dead young lover. The ancient "philosopher" was a craggy aphorist who wore a threadbare but clean suit and clicked his heels when introduced, and whose "philosophy" I found idiotic. The leather-jacketed fop became my friend Adrian, and one of the high schoolers was my future love, Aurelia. A committee of five portly men (the judges) sat above us at a red-cloth-draped dais on a platform. Behind them hung framed lithographs of the Fathers of Communism: Marx, Engels, Lenin, Stalin, and Gheorghiu-Dej, so each judge sat under his own lithographed "father." The plaster moulding running around the salon ceiling was broken at intervals by chipped putti that had once been gilded but had since become poxed by leaking rain. I looked up at them often to keep myself from looking at the Workshop judges who narcotized me from their very first remarks, making me drift into a hypnagogic state I had difficulty returning from. The proceedings began after the judges introduced themselves each session, providing, in addition to their credentials, an addendum of the rules of decorum we needed to observe, which included unswerving loyalty to the working class and the Communist Party. The Workshop Chairman sat at the center of the group in a winged chair, with an open notebook and an uncapped fountain pen before him. He took "the minutes." (Where he took them was supposed to be a mystery, but everyone knew that he took them one floor up to the office of a bald man with a rheumy eye who was the city's "ideological instructor" and censor.) One floor above the censor was the editorial office of the Party's weekly paper, *Flacăra Sibiului* (*Sibiu's Flame*), and one floor above that, at the very top, was the ballroom-size office of the First Secretary of Sibiu's Communist Party regional branch. The Secretary was still young, restless, and not from town, and we often spoke our verses louder to cover his earth-shaking grunts when he made love to his secretary on Baron von Bruckenthal's desk. These occasions were sources of great hilarity for us high schoolers, we barely kept from bursting out laughing, but the stern faces of the judges reminded us quickly that half of our families were or had been in prison for just such impertinences. I'd been to every room in the place with my father, and I knew that they became increasingly more refined on each floor: the Censor's ceiling displayed nymphs and fawns with lyres, while the Secretary's was fully equipped with bronze busts of Johann Sebastian Bach, Baron von Bruckenthal, Martin Luther, and Michelangelo, as well as the ubiquitous lithographs of Marx, Engels, Lenin, Stalin and Gheorghe

Gheorghiu-Dej. I pictured to myself the mighty desk that broadcast the Secretary's groans, and it was even harder for me than for my colleagues from bursting into merriment. What was even funnier to me, beyond knowing the exact layout of the room, was that I knew that Baron von Bruckenthal had invented torture instruments, including the rack™, and had hosted celebrated 18th-century Viennese composers in his art-festooned salon. The idea that all this pompous culture was being violated by a grunting apparachik from Bucharest was funny to me for reasons I couldn't explain then, but I suspect that the pomposity of the Workshop writers' poetry mixed like snuff powder with my recall of the room. My mother, who could be quite acidic at times, may have also called the Secretary "a rube in pee-stained breeches," which didn't help. I trace my legendary ability to keep a straight face to this superhuman effort not to laugh in the Workshop, though I developed a rictus from the effort, a face-spasm that took years to overcome. Across the street from our building, Bruckenthal Museum sheltered the Baron's art, to which the communists had added their own wing dedicated to the "history of the Romanian Communist party." Our school conducted an obligatory lunar outing to it, to view paintings of sweaty but happy peasants holding sheafs of grain, bare-chested steel workers pouring molten metal into huge vats and, above all, the pride of the collection: a life-scale bronze sculpture of Lenin atop a train locomotive at the Finland station in Petrograd with his arm outstretched, greeted by an ecstatic mob of bronze proletarians. Outside of school groups, nobody ever came here voluntarily. Behind Lenin on his locomotive was the ideal hiding place where Aurelia first showed me hers and I showed her mine. For a detailed and prurient description of this scene, including the sudden contraction of the bronze wrinkles in Lenin's neck, see my memoir *The Life & Times of An Involuntary Genius* (George Braziller, 1975).

Each Wednesday evening, the Writers' Workshop dedicated itself to the work of a writer who had signed up to recite original work and submit to criticism. The best part of this performance was toward the end, when the performer, after reading the work and suffering the arrows and stinging wit of the others, offered herm's own "self-criticism," a summary of lessons learned from the arrows and stings. A writer might be lucky enough to come up twice before the workshop judges and the audience, but here, as elsewhere in the workers' state, strings could be pulled: it was thus that I heard more than my fair share of episodes from the doctor's epic that might still be going on if the Iron Curtain hadn't rusted. The doctor who penned this ouvrage pulled every string in his power (renowned local salamis wrapped individually for each judge) to take extra turns. Most of us were poets, but the doctor was a novelist. It was generally understood that a novel was a lifetime kind of business, undertaken only in middle age by the most substantial citizens; the doctor's round belly was traversed by the chain of a bourgeois vest-pocket watch, while his vast epic depicted the class struggles of hundreds of characters yearning for communism. It was in no way an eccentric work; multi-volume novels of this type, inspired by Sholokov's *Quiet Flows the Don* were regularly dispatched in millions of copies to the proletariat. They were never read, but they shared places of honor on barrack shelves with mostly empty bottles of plum brandy. "You know why the proletariat dictates?" went the joke, "Because it can't write." "The dictatorship of the proletariat" was on the receiving end of a waterfall of educational prose. Men like the doctor, backed by the fire-power of salamis produced by their peasant kin, used the medium to achieve glory, without anyone having read a word of what they wrote. (This, in a slightly different variation, is also the case in capitalism, but more about that later.)

Poetry was the medium of choice for young auditors like myself, who were too young to have acquired enough "experience" for a novel, but many of us also had "unhealthy social origins." Mine was *petit bourgeois*, an origin not as unhealthy as *chiabur* (pig-owning sausage provider), but unhealthy enough to place me at the bottom of any list that was headed by *workers* and *peasants* whose "healthy origins" meant that no one in their families, as far as known, had ever owned anything or gone to school. A complete lack of accomplishments was the background of the tabula rasa that would, ideally, propel the heirs of nothingness to inherit the earth. In the Writers' Workshop there were many participants with "unhealthy origins," which is why everyone tried very hard to prove allegiance to the "brilliant" system, and why we were faithfully reported to the Censor by the Workshop Chairman. (The excessively zealous also reported each other to the same source.) Each week's chosen writer, holding tightly herm sheaf of literary work, climbed up on the stage to the right of the judges, who turned their chairs to look at herm. When the coughs and harumphing and scraping of chair legs subsided, the supplicant shuffled herm papers and read original compositions in a tiny voice or, as in the case of the doctor, one as stentorian as a deadly diagnosis. The versifiers' verses were conventional, as were the critiques, the judge's summations, and the self-critique, but the doctor's novel served up endless pretexts for demonstrating ideological correctness. Unfinished, this novel will now lie undisturbed in the official Archives of communism for one thousand years. At the end of that time, God will let Satan out of his chains at the bottom of the well, and we will all be compelled to hear it again.

When I first started attending the Workshop, I felt small and intimidated, and I was politely attentive. Slowly however, between the awfulness of the writing and the grunts of the Party secretary, I suppressed my swelling hilarity by imagining unfunny things, like dreadful and horrendously painful tortures applied to the droning asses on stage with the aid of Baron von Bruckenthal's devices. The scenes behind my mask were vivid and seditious, and if I returned briefly from my bone-crushing travels and caught some insanely amusing conceit emanating from a performer, I used the last resort available to me, short of peeing my pants and bursting out in uncontrollable giggles: I killed my mother. (This turned out to be a useful imaginary tool later, too, to keep myself from prematurely ejaculating.) The doctor was the one performer egregious enough to override even my saddest thought. I had to block all of him or risk perdition. In the "newly opened archives" of the Romanian Communist Party, there are numerous black and white photographs of small groups of people listening "enraptured" to a man on a podium reading "original literary work," and among these there is certainly a copy of the *Sibiu Flame* displaying on its front page a grainy photograph of the proceedings of the 1961 Sibiu Writers' Workshop, in which a discerning eye might find a young blob with closed eyes, about to explode, behind whose eyelids pass endless images of matricide, torture on the rack™, and Aurelia's thighs carelessly open. With poets I could take the chance now and then of leaving behind my flow of laughter-strangling images, but with the doctor there was no escape. My occasional encounters with the poets' pronouncements were sufficient to conceive instantly a deadly critique of their work, which I started offering with some enjoyment. The shocking encounter between my deliberate daydreaming and the reality of a few lines in a live performance had the effect of a concentrated dose of smelling salts, an effect I retain to this day. If a performance is exceedingly boring my daydreaming is usually safe, but if a slightly obligatory gesture is called for, I can tune in the exact moment when the most egregious stupidity is being displayed, and I find instantly the words to (critically) describe it... Encountering reality while in midst of an inner movie is unpleasant but I am a deadly shot when I fire at reality at its point of intrusion. I've had filmic masterpieces wrecked by a stage quip and took revenge, accordingly. When our Workshop readers were through with their nerve-wracking hour, the auditors stood stock still, and allowed a few seconds of respectful silence before they began to raise their hands. A raised hand was called upon by a judge, and the auditor stood, bowed to the performer, and proceeded to remark on what herm had just heard, a critique followed by a preamble assessing the reader's political "awareness" of "the working class." I was still at the beginning of my poetry studies, so I hadn't yet become imbued with the full religion of poetry which requires, I now know, the miming of a respectful silence. It was assumed and never mentioned that every person was two people: a public one who smiled and lied, and a private one who cursed and cried. (Sing it!) That was the reality we inhabited, the touchingly simple world of socialism & schizophrenia. I knew that newspapers lied worse than people, and people lied for a living. In public they lied just like newspapers and the speakers at our school assemblies, lying had its own language, specially created for The Big Lie. The Big Lie was chiefly the opposite of what anyone felt at any given moment, the imperative of compulsory optimism, an easily recognizable and universally feared language. The existence of such a monolithic lie made it easy to ignore. If you were suicidal or stupid (the same thing) you could test your ideas by setting them up against the Big Lie. If what you said was the opposite of the Big Lie, you were obviously right, but if you were in your right mind you kept it to yourself, or you went straight to prison or the insane asylum. Of course, this made it easy to have ideas, because they stood out so well against the background. In the end, the Big Lie was not as monolithic as it seemed: many of its formulations seeped into our psyches and made themselves home because it was futile to oppose them. I took it for granted, for instance, that all people on earth share a common interest in justice because Marx said so. But whatever the Big Lie was it wasn't literature. In the Writing Workshop, the Big Lie sat Cerberus-like at the dais, and speakers addressed their introductory perfunctory remarks to it, but it was also clear that although they sounded alike at first, the participants belonged to opposite camps: they divided along traditionalist or modernist lines. The traditionalists wrote rhymed romantic pastiches of the canonized classics, while the modernists wrote blank verse that dared to mention machines and cities; the traditionalists relied on the sure-fire reflexes stamped in us by our scholastic tradition of memorizing long pastoral-cataclysmic ballads, while the modernists read the rare issues of literary weeklies from Bucharest and found out, mostly in translation, that there were other kinds of poets out there. It appeared also that writers in the capital were (delicately) breaking out of the confines of socialist-realism, like the Rembrandt-school painting of the beauties testing the water in a spring with their naked toes. A poet named Nicolae Labiş, who had taken his pen-name from the French for "fawn," though otherwise a "healthy-origin" proletarian, had broken the mould with nouveau symbolist rhymes that failed to mention the proletariat. It was as if Labiş had suddenly lifted the heavy iron lid of the box where the commies had stashed all the metaphors: young poets dove in. There were even literary critics in the reawakened capital who declared that the only poet capable of such a feat was one with impeccable proletarian credentials, like Labiş. Party lapdogs like Mihai Beniuc, who had begun as a modernist in the dark days of the bourgeoisie, had voluntarily surrendered their metaphors to the strongbox Labiş opened, and now that he had opened it, young whipper-snappers swarmed to it like a stew made with real meat. Proletcultism was suddenly out of fashion. The swarm of hungry poets descending on the dried meat of the surrendered avantgarde took over the Transylvanian weekly *Steaua* (*The Star*) and the Bucharest weekly *Luceafărul* (*The Evening Star*). Communist propaganda never strayed far from "stars," "sparks" and "flames." In those blinding rhetorical lights one was supposed to discern the shape of "the new man" of the future. But now, suddenly and mysteriously, one could discern right alongside the communist Frankenstein a series of unapproved figures. Occasionally, one of the distant young deities from Cluj or Bucharest descended on our Workshop with a hunk of meat from the image trunk. At their public readings, there were no critiques, only applause. We pubescent poets boiled with excitement at the fresh air that clung to the visitors, the air of late-night debates about poetry in smoky cafes. (Fresh air in the Age of the First Sixties Awakening was smoky.) Our staid locals were not pleased, but they didn't fuss: after all, even incorrect, the visitors were from the capital, and the capital must be respected by the province no matter what.

By the time I was scheduled to present my work on the dais, I was already a veteran at critiquing my elders: I fancied myself the agent of poetry's fresh air, a merciless ironist and herald of liberty to come. I zeroed in on the weaknesses and pretensions of my colleagues' careful sentences and demolished them like sand castles. My hand was the first one up, and up it stayed until I was called on. I then opened fire. The traditionalists called my speeches "chutzpah," a well-intended slur, while the crypto-modernists weren't quite sure how to handle my offhanded unveiling of their obscure intentions. I always began by stripping the work of the obligatory rhetoric, a distinct blow below the belt. The introductory rhetoric was understood as the necessary paean to the Party and its glorious ideology, but not as crudely as all that – all one had to do to dispense with the paean in the early Sixties, after Stalin died, was to use a few key words such as "bricks," "towers," "peaks," "pine-scent" or "the new man," and then get on with the business at hand, which was the work of the "Comrade writer" under discussion. It was considered very bad etiquette to draw attention to the preamble, which was, as in ages past, a simple dedication to the noble patron who paid for the printing. In the near past, the patron had been no other than Stalin himself, but as his body started slowly decomposing, his name disintegrated likewise into numerous euphemisms. One didn't need to weep while speaking His name, but it was required that speakers expend at least a few words about "the new man," because they were "creative," and they were expected to envision this "new man." It was for the sake of this "new man" (blond, muscular, holding a scythe or a rifle, proficient with a combine, intimate with a tractor and equally at home with a test tube) that the masses starved, that the workers sacrificed. The high schoolers rolled their eyes when "the new man" came up: he sounded like a god and a robot, and I once made Aurelia literally pee in her panties when, during one of the workshoppers' "new man" rants, I slipped her a drawing of this god-robot with a huge erection. The word "robot" was from the Slavic for "labor:" We labored to make a perfect laborer in our utopian future, an erect one. I knew that the weakness of writing being committed in the Writers' Workshop, if not in the entirety of "the socialist camp," was neither more nor less than this introductory paean, which was the substance of permitted expression, no matter what followed it or who the speaker was. Despite its seemingly inoffensive product, the Workshop was a battleground for status, its influence extending far beyond the House of Culture. Citizens who were praised in the Workshop rose in their own esteem, as well as of that of their superiors; the battleground of literary endeavor was as bloody as any battleground. One would no more march forth without the standard of a flying paean into a world threatened by career-failure than a knight would march without a flying cross flag into Jerusalem. In this, the writers of the year 1961 were united, traditionalists no less than modernists. Everyone knew that the paean was not to be touched, a delicate maneuver that licensed a critic to dwell on everything except what was in front of herm nose. The payoff for correctly reciting the paean was often immediate: poets could wear velvet sleeves, longer hair, a dirty shirt, a pencil-thin moustache, or, introduce a peculiar intonation, accent, or neologism into their poetry.

My personal revolution and subsequent repression started when I ignored this agreement and used all the naive charm of my tender youth to attack all compositions at their most vulnerable point: the Paean. It was a Cliché, I said (memorably). There were others who were avowed enemies of the Cliché (often disguised as an Adjective), but they were never so impolite as to identify the paean itself with a Cliché. The Paean, I continued, was not just any Cliché, but **the** Cliché. I had the excuse of my youth, of course, but I was instantly suspected of being a Shrewd Jew, another Cliché that I deconspired as soon as adjectives like Shrewd, Canny, Clever started showing up in the outraged rebuttals to my chutzpah. The angry rebuttals that starred the Shrewd Jew were going with the flow of the antisemitism of Stalin's last years, still flowing, albeit more sluggishly, in the post-stalinist era. We had an entire antisemitic language, with an extensive vocabulary that didn't even need the word "jew" or "kike" to swell with blood-lust. It was from this vocabulary that I drew my first pseudonym: *Steiu*. Andrei Steiu was born at an onomastic session of the Writers' Workshop in 1962. It was a special session that an entire weekly meeting had been dedicated to without my knowledge. The Workshop Chairman announced that the evening's agenda was "facilitating the publication of Andrei Perlmutter's work." (Everyone knew that with a name like "Perlmutter" one would never grace the pages of a Romanian literary weekly.) I was startled, but not surprised: the nonexistence of racial prejudice was one of the tenets of the Big Lie. Various names were butted about, but I wasn't going to let them rename me, so I joined the game by shouting out loud the most outrageously sincere rustic words from the antisemitic vocabulary. "Steiu," which is what I finally named myself, means "peak," or "crag," or "mountain top," a place so pure and high and jagged no Jew had ever been there. (The Big Lie's code for Jews was "cosmopolitans," and it was known from that that they lived only in cities, where they never breathed in deeply the mountain air or beheld the beauty of nature. The Big Lie was beginning to suffer nationalist modifications shortly before Kruschev de-stalinized Russia, and one of those was the relocation of "Jews" on the ideological map, to unhealthy city ghettoes, and the re-appropriation of nature—such as it was after the heavy industrial pollution of the Five-Year Plans—by "pure" ethnics.) My nom-de-plume satisfied my confreres until it was realized that in signing my new name I was obliged by our cursive handwriting style to make the "u" resemble an "n," which turned "Steiu" into "Stein," a word also meaning "rock," but in German, and a Jewish name at that. It wasn't until I found "Codrescu" that I hit the deepest chord of nationalist gore, but that was long after 1962. (You can find the story in *The Life & Times of An Involuntary Genius.*) I wish I remembered some of the names other writers suggested for me back then, but I am certain that they came from the (secretly ironic) vocabulary of proletcultist metaphors: pines, raised chins, clenched fists, giant leaps, and celestial vaults with bright stars, sparks and flames. (The brighter the metaphor, the darker the reality, and as reality darkened considerably in decades to come, nearly all public language was engulfed in happy flames of rhetorica obscura.) In 1962, even freshly baptized, I did not tow the line: I kept up my antics in the critique part of the program, and I even made converts: Adrian, my elder leather-jacketed pal who was already a published poet, and Aurelia, who wrote tiny timid stories and whose body I ardently longed for. The Tuesday after my baptism I was supposed to present my work in the Workshop, but I already suspected that the critique would be a bloodbath, so my friends prepared to defend me. Adrian, Aurelia and I sat up until closing time at the Golden Barrel going over the poems in my not-yet-lost notebook, deciding which ones were the most defensible and the least impeachable. They all contained a measure of religiosity, decadence and profanity, so there was no turning back from that, and we ended up choosing the most religious, decadent, and profane work because Adrian quoted Napoleon to the effect that offense is the best defense. The most outrageous lyric announced in one verse that "the red cow has ceased giving milk." This unspeakably offensive line (I know, you had to be there!) was well-embedded in an otherwise agriculturalist set of images of wheat, bread and happy sweat in regular slanted rhyme. You really *did* have to be there to see the effect this verse had: the novelling doctor nearly toppled backwards in his chair... three judges raised their eyes to the ceiling to looked through it in search of help from a higher power... there was consternation, indignation, disbelief... the love poet went into orgasmic convulsions... the hunter squeezed a medal in his pocket and blood stained his pants... I had dealt a deadly blow to the regime with a symbol! A bovine symbol. A red and white symbol. The ship of state listed starboard. The consequences were short-term and long-term. I wrote about the long-term consequences in *The Life & Times of An Involuntary Genius*, most memorably the disciplinary encounter with the First Secretary of the Communist Party of Sibiu. I did not dwell there on the short-term, but I'll confess now that what followed my raw metaphorical burst (that included the sterilized cow) was an awed silence. It could have been a sigh of wariness, or, as I chose to interpret it, the recognition that a new beast had arrived in the woods and, while it was probably prudent to kill it instantly, one couldn't help but be moved by its beauty. The writers in the room, even the stupidest among them, knew in their gut the difference between a cuckoo clock and a real cuckoo. Most of them had never heard a real cuckoo, except for the hunter in the bleeding pants, but they

That poets were valued and watched by the authorities did not escape me: I hoped to be valued and watched (and hopefully punished) for my poetic transgressions.

The communists, and all intellectuals, were book people. The ideology itself had spread from dank underground print shops through inflammatory pamphlets. The founders' pamphlets, now books gilded and bound, were required furniture for party apparachiks.[6] The Communist party employed censors and monitored an index more extensive than the Vatican's. Children's first outing was to the library, and while the Bible and lots of other books were forbidden, the object itself was worshipped. Astra, the oldest library in Sibiu, housed Gutenberg-era books, some of them printed right in our burg. Some of them were Bibles, and most of them treated religious subjects inspired by the Bible. We were rarely told what they were about, and, since they were in Latin anyway, few librarians knew themselves. From elementary school through high school we were herded in to view them: huge books, chained to pulpits, open to hand-painted miniatures or fine engravings. We stood around them in a circle, while a librarian turned a page or two. The librarians were young, recruited from "the ranks of the

were certain that the kid facing them was an animal, not a robot. They all aspired, to some degree, to be both robotic and human, that is to say mechanical and animal, but they hadn't thought it possible to be so defiantly animal. This is when Aurelia fell in love with me. The mumbles that followed were awkward excuses to change the subject, and there was even feint praise for my "musicality," from the love poetess. My friends did not have to defend me publicly, which was just as well. Most of the people who said nothing denounced me next day to the Censor as a subversive and dangerous reactionary, which led to the long-term consequences discussed in *The Life & Times*... But the chief short-term consequence is that Aurelia let me kiss her full on the lips and run my hand under her silky soutienne and feel the iron contraption that held her breasts. We drank so much after my triumph that after being thus rewarded, I walked straight into a telephone pole like a cartoon character and sported a purple egg on my forehead for a week. In some way, all future writing workshop experiences, the few I attended and the many I taught, were contained inside that purple egg.

[6] Attention thesis-subject hunters: a pamphlet becomes a book when the author comes to power and has minions stuff it with "science," in this case "dialectical materialism." Most of these books were burned or trashed after 1989, but a few of them were used by the artist Ciprian Mureşan to make a round Romanian water-well, traditional in peasant villages: the spines face outward and the rounded insides are garnished with broken mirrors; the bottom is a mirror, so that when viewed from above, the installation is an infinite well. The unsettling horror of what flows out of it is not speculative: this is the well of textuality gone haywire. Mureşan's work with books as objects commenting on contemporary life and ideas continue into the "new, capitalist" Romania: in one of them a shopping cart full of used books appears abandoned on the street. The shopping cart is the new Romania, the books (discarded) the old.

working class," which meant that they had been hastily trained to deliver a spiel about the items on display. They had also learned important things. Dirty hands, for instance, especially the dirty hands of children, were the equivalent of an uprising. Their own hands, recently freed from working the soil or maintaining tanks in the army, were painfully scrubbed. When our class entered the sanctum their eyes zeroed in on our hands. The showing did not begin until every hand was lined to the side of every body. When the librarian was certain that our grubby paws knew their place, we were shown the books with woodcuts, copper-plate engravings, and ornate Latin script. The books smelled strange, they had an oddly arousing scent, bitter like unshelled walnut. I sometimes encounter this smell in an old library and it transports me instantly to Astra. On one occasion, we were showed Astra's greatest treasure: a 16th-century incunabulum that displayed the impression of a single page of the manuscript of *Tristan and Isolde* of Gottfried von Strassburg, written in 1213. The page from *Tristan and Isolde* that had been used in the leather binding had long since disappeared, leaving behind only its traces in the leather. The librarian made a de facto presentation of this rarity, and then she explained why such a miraculous object was among us. She said that just as the ancient manuscript page had left its script in the leather, the ancient Romans and Dacians, the ancestors of the Romanian people today, had left their traces in us. I had no trouble understanding how the Roman legionnaires who raped the local Dacian women had left their traces in the current us, and how the Dacians and the ancient Romans, having disappeared from history, now only existed in us. This is also what we were told in school. We displayed

7 The first book Gutenberg published using movable type was the Bible, but the second was a pamphlet with gruesome illustrations, commissioned by the burghers of Sibiu to publicize the atrocities of Prince Dracula who sacked the town and impaled some of its best citizens. The Dracula pamphlet with its vivid woodcuts had a phenomenal and instant impact: it was translated in many countries, including Russia, where it inspired Ivan the Terrible. Gutenberg's second printed book was the world's first best-seller: the gory horror story lasted centuries, until it flowed into Bram Stoker's *Dracula*, a novel that  eclipsed Gutenberg's thriller, and gave us the chief figure of the modern immortal (who wears a tux while he sucks, unlike the Prince who wore a spiked collar and had zero table manners). Technology propagated this story out of rude historical half-truths to mythical heights, but the price was loss of manners (i.e., democracy). Bram Stoker described in his introduction that *Dracula* was cobbled together from a "mass of typewriting" dictated to the fictional Mina Harker. I read somewhere that some scholars see this as an allegory of the vampiric nature of modern communications media. But the vampire *adds* life like Coke, so the soul-stealing hint in that allegory doesn't hold.

the traces of vanished ancients like the lost page from *Tristan and Isolde*, we were a binding impressed with sacred script. This became a metaphor for my destiny: I felt that leaving the traces of one's passage, in even such attenuated form, was worth the labor of a lifetime.

Our town had housed one of the oldest printing guilds in Europe, contemporary with Gutenberg; it was exclusively German, a guild that my mother (non-German, but German-speaking, and skilled) eventually joined in 1962 to become a color separator. My mother's belonging to this tradition was a matter of secret pride to me, just as my deliberate mockery of "tradition" was my public stand.[7] The unlined notebook, sworn to secrecy, ranged freely between pride and scorn. I kept nothing from it. Outside the notebook the prosaic world provided me only with proofs for my feelings: my crushes ("great loves" in those days), fantasies of revenge against my stepfather, hatred of school, satire of the Workshop, and oedipal conundrums were all transcribed into the notebook, sketches for a philosophy or a poetics without much detail, but rich in vehemence. Rehearsing my Nobel Prize acceptance speech, for instance, was mostly an inward affair, but echoes of its most brilliant formulations found their way into the notebook. I discovered in the attic of our apartment building several trunks predating the war, possibly the 20th century; inside one of them was a splendidly bound set of Austrian encyclopedias with shiny thick paper and lush illustrations. I read them greedily, forgetting even that the German they were written in was quite different from the pedestrian German I spoke with Peter Albrecht next door. Another trunk contained brand new top hats like the ones worn by evil capitalists in our schoolbooks. These majestic, shiny head-thrones came wrapped in silk inside round boxes. My Nobel Prize acceptance speech had the gravitas of the Austrian encyclopedias and the authority of top hats. For all that, the aggressive and vengeful nature of the speech itself drew its energy mostly from raw anger against my practically illiterate stepfather, a train conductor with whom I shared a dreadful secret: his mandatory copy of Stalin's treatise on railroads was also bought at Kniga Ruskaya where my notebook came from.

Denying the source of the notebook was a full time job for a budding poet and protodissident, so all my "poetic" excuses and odd behavior were intensified. If people had found me distracted before the unlined notebook, they now found me insufferable. Adolescence is a time of life to be endured by all concerned, but when coupled with a "calling," such as "poet," it can be dangerous, liable to become permanent, and a threat to society. All of this was outlined in the unlined notebook, and if the unlined notebook is ever found it will be full of clues about my primal muck. Unfortunately, just as I was beginning to feel that my notes and poetry were gaining density and becoming inhabited by a spirit that I could think of as "mine," I lost it. Tragedy. I cringe, even at a distance of half a century, at the magnitude of the loss. Crushed, I dragged myself through the empty streets, sure that I was going mad like the syphilitic national genius Mihai Eminescu. I sometimes thought that it had been stolen by one of my mediocre poetic rivals, and I did entertain briefly the idea that it had been taken by some volatile ghost to heaven where its words were weighed to decide my fate (which, in a funny way, is exactly what happened).

In the absence of my first archive, I could either give up writing and become a "decent" proletarian, or I could begin anew by diversifying, in which case the loss of a single notebook didn't mean the end of my pleasure in writing.

The heavens decreed that I should diversify. I started by trying to reproduce the original. I wrote again all the poems I remembered in a new notebook (available by this time at the regular stationary store, making a risky foray to the hated Soviet shop unnecessary). This legit notebook was unsatisfactory, without a touch of derring-do and rehearsed besides; my poetry felt tamed.[8] The notes were gone, alas, and copying my memorized verses did not reassure me. If I lost *this* notebook, my inspiration was sure to be recalled. Producing multiple copies was not easy in a country where every typewriter was registered with the police. My two girlfriends agreed to copy my work by hand on the back of their Romanian literature textbooks, but extracted a heavy price from me, not just in terms of their increased demand for attention, but also in the subtle but soul-shattering ways in which they forced me to self-censor. The poems I handed them contained subtle modifications, visible to no one but myself, I'm sure, but containing even in their invisibility possible hints of favoring one girl over another. Compromise reared its Medusa head. The lazier copyist was generous with her body, while my other fan was industrious but cerebral. Consequently, my poems behaved differently in each of their hands, even when the words looked, outwardly, to someone else, exactly the same.

[8] It is surprising how many degrees of tameness were available for comparison in my dusty provincial town.

An allegory of sorts came, in the form of both poetic reproduction and sex, one rainy afternoon in my friend Adrian's room. Adrian, my older poet friend from the Workshop, had a leather jacket and a mysterious job. He put his huge manual Underwood typewriter at my disposal one Friday when he left town on one of his mysterious errands. This mind-blowing act of faith could mean only that Adrian thought that I was a genius whose time had come to type. (Or else, retrospectively, that he was representing the occult poetry arm of Securitate, the secret police, which was prudently collecting precocious geniuses for later uses.) Alone with the huge machine, fingers poised... but let me quote the exact passage from my book, *The Hole in the Flag* (William Morrow, 1991), where I did a better job of marking this moment:

*I intended to type all the poems from the overflowing notebook. But just as I flexed my fingers, there was a knock at the door. I opened it and there was Betty, twenty-two years old, with a brown cardboard suitcase. She had, it seems, met Adrian on a train, and he'd told her to come visit when she found herself in the big city. There she was, with a kerchief on her hair and big dark eyes. I bade her to make herself at home, and I resumed my important work. But I couldn't concentrate. Every time I succeeded in typing a word I would steal a glance at the girl lying on the bed with her arms under her head, watching me. Her breasts rose and fell in time to her breathing but not in time to my typing, though at first I did try to match them. In the struggle between my waning desire to type and my growing desire to touch her breasts, my future personality was being formed. It appeared that I was not yet ready to make the transition from the dreamy intimacy of handwriting to the metallic responsibility of public domain. It also appeared that I was not courageous enough to leap on Betty's breasts. On the other hand, I might have summoned the courage had Adrian not come home. He found me with my handwritten poems staring helplessly from my notebook and his future wife asleep on the bed. The typewriter lay untouched, as did Betty.*

*Further attempts at typing that year were fruitless as well because every time I began to touch the keys I would strain my ear for a knock on the door. It was not until I left Romania that I could sit at a typewriter and just type, as if it were a normal thing to do. By then things had changed. I liked the staccato din of American life. I liked the typewriterlike hum of New York and its rushing humans, who looked to me like the madly dancing keys of a shiny, vast keyboard. America moved at the speed of its keyboards. I began composing directly on the typewriter. Knocks on the door, when they came, did not break my concentration. Au contraire, I used the excitement to spur me to greater heights of typing. Whenever I thought of my sad Romania, I thought of registered typewriters, forbidden copiers, a place where writing was deemed more dangerous than bombs, a place of sadness, silence, handwriting, and the shyness of boy geniuses.*

Throughout the entire saga—of my early writings in Romanian, my emigration to America, my learning of English, my first poems, readings and then publications in the United States—I always carried notebooks.

If one wasn't handy, as was the case briefly in Italy in 1965, when I was in transit to the US[9], I used other people's books to jot my notes around the print. In Italy I used for a notebook a book by a poet named Renata Pescanti Botti, ideal because I wrote my poetry in the wide vacant spaces around Renata's poems. When I ran out of room I also wrote and drew over Renata's verses. I dragged this book with me from Rome to New York, both because it had become an interesting object and because I wanted to eventually extract my poems from it. I lost it at the Figaro Cafe at Bleecker and MacDougal. By then I carried a cloth satchel full of notebooks. Each notebook served a different function, according to a vast and now mostly forgotten plan to create poetic personae who looked at the world in different ways, and in different languages. I think that I was writing a sort of novel in verse, trying out characters for my new American life. I wasn't trying to be someone else, I was just testing creatures that might charm the girls and threaten the bad guys. I was inventing a "self" with all the luxury of choice my twenty years gave me; I was like a newborn who could read and write; weaving together mythologies of exile and rebirth was my work. I knew that I had moved to another country where the natives spoke a language I didn't know, but the substance of what I meant to be in any language was *poet*. Languages, geography or poverty didn't matter. Those obstacles were to be leapt over playfully (hopefully) or painfully (if necessary). Whenever I looked around

[9] Rome, Naples and Vienna were transit points for Romanian emigrants headed for Israel and West Germany. The waiting period was usually six months, until the host country issued an entry permit. Most emigrants tried desperately to reach the US and Canada, but they had little chance if they didn't have someone sponsoring them. The "refugee camp" my mother and I stayed in was actually a fairly decent apartment building in a "bad" part of Rome; Mossad agents and, I suppose, their West German counterparts, gave daily lectures with slides about the wonders of Israel and West Germany, in an attempt to convince us to go to where we were supposed to go. Happily, we had a sponsor in the United States: my high school math teacher who had emigrated to Detroit some years earlier, and still carried a torch for my mother.

me I saw young and beautiful people like myself frowning deeply over their own notebooks, deeply absorbed by the existential and sexy terrors of creative labor. I absorbed them and their thoughts, and transferred them whole to my world; I imported them into my notebooks. I'm emphatic here to prevent any humorless exegete reading my self-mythologizing youthful tales from thinking that I was shedding identities like a snake to fool the goodhearted natives. I had come to America with a sack full of identities: Jewish, Romanian, Transylvanian, Dacian, Roman, poet, reader. I was a grab-bag of defiant persons. My mythology wasn't intended to fool anyone. I was deadly serious. I was hoping to share some of the wealth of my "selves" with people my age, and thus barter my way into my new country. I was at war with any identity that thought itself as permanent, and I was determined to reveal such abundance of identities that the idea of identity itself would seem absurd.[10]

I meant to make people laugh because they saw the abyss looking back at them from my poems, as Nietzsche almost said. I wanted to see their terror turn into surprise and shocked laughter, and then we

[10] The idea that a sole "identity" should be opposed came later, when I applied for US citizenship and found out that I had an FBI file, and that the process of vetting me via this folder would take years. Alas. The folder was lost twice (like my notebooks): once by the FBI agent who retired before he compiled it all, and a second time by an agency that borrowed it and never returned it. I never learned the name of the borrowing agency, but a folder did reappear at the time of my final "examination" in 1981. Using FOIA I later sued to see this folder and was sent a tiny sheaf of papers about one-tenth the size of the one I'd seen on my INS agent's desk. There is a motif here linking my lost notebooks (written by me) with my lost folders (written by others), and the fact that my second "lost" book was found, just as was my second official report (though much diminished by redaction). For a fuller story, see *In America's Shoes* (City Lights Books, 1983). Until I applied for citizenship (in order to get a passport so I could leave the country and come back) I didn't think much about national identity. I assumed that "internationalism" was a fait-accompli, in the sense that all the people in the world were friends, which is what we were taught in school. The reality of Romanian nationalism, obvious as daylight outside of school, made no impression on me; I was certain of my place within "the family of nations," a family symbolized by my German friend Peter, my Romanian friend Ion, and my Hungarian pal Jossi. It never occurred to me that all these variously-tongued pals were Romanian *citizens*, a weighty fact backed by wars, treaties, and rivers of blood. When prickly pedestrian antisemitic moments came my way, I took them for friendly ribbing. I mean what is a gawky Jewish boy wearing glasses in Romania, without jokes about his provenance and figure? I was aware of some obscure imbalance (the ribbing was sometimes disproportionate to my human flaws) but I took it well, striving to become more flawed, to meet the insulting expectations. Didn't I speak *all* the languages of my city's nationals? What I didn't know was that the same jokes had been told a decade earlier when the Jewish boy with glasses was taken to a death camp and killed. I didn't know that there

was a difference between a citizen and an ethnic, the latter being subject to a continuous pressure to assert power over the other ethnics. I believed in the "brotherhood of nations" because I didn't know history, not even the history of my school where the teaching of "race purity" one decade before the Second World War had preceded the teaching of marxist "internationalism." A chasm opened in the Fifties in the confusion of the transition between ideologies. Old teachers, as well as slow learners (which included the indifferent) were not fast enough to notice that "ethnicity" was made secondary to "nationality," and that "nationality" was placed below the "golden future of humanity," i.e., communism. These old and slow learners fell into the chasm: prison, silence, blackmail. Only school children like myself moved forward without the terror of windowless black vans following them, and only a clueless Jew like myself (and there were only three of us in Sibiu by 1963) could absorb the optimism of brotherly love propaganda without noticing that all my friends' families had missing members and a diffuse suspicion of foreign-language speakers. I had no father, but mine had evanesced for psychological reasons, not evaporated by history like the fathers of my friends. On the other hand, or side, all my grandmother's sisters and children were seized by Hungarian authorities and exterminated at Auschwitz. Maybe I wouldn't have liked Jossi so much if I'd known that. But the communists passed over those still-open wounds in silence, they induced a chasm of amnesia that they stuffed with the ideology of the "brotherhood of nations." Now, should I be grateful to the Archives of Amnesia that is the dark twin of History, or should I rue its existence? This is the question that still haunts us, long after the end of the Cold War: does the history of the vanquished, written out of the Official Archives, be set back into the light and on the same footing as the Official Archives? Only a callous vampire would say NO, but if the answer is YES, which is how liberal humanists have answered since the end of the Second World War, what is to be done about the inevitable anger, horror, and helplessness that follows the restoration? The South African "reconciliation" policy may provide the Christian answer, but forgiveness, as good a principle as "internationalism," will hardly be making a Christ out of every schmo. In 1963-1964, my last years of high school, there was occasional talk of "mistakes" and "corrections" in the internationalist doctrine, but I thought that they were usually made in order to patch it up, like repairing shoes. I now know that they were small signals from the Romanian Communist Party preparing for the post-stalinist era. My ability (or blindness) to see no contradiction between the ideal and the real, or between reality and lies, was made possible by the silence of our elders, who told us nothing about their past. Everyone's past was in some measure suspect (even if they'd belonged to an underground communist cell; the commies eliminated each other with greater efficiency than their worst enemies), so most people preferred silence. The tight-lipped Saxon culture of Sibiu was traditionally silent, so what few words we heard were mostly banter, at the limit of which the only hint that not all was well, were jokes. Jokes opposed the official lies through irrefutable paradoxes. Another hint that a disconnect ran through what we saw and what we heard were fairy tales. The ease with which the impossible took place in these stories mirrored the ease (or eased the anxiety) with which we were capable of living the reality and the lie simultaneously. In a magical world, things that contradicted one another just happened, and their heroes survived through supernatural intervention. The citizens of communist Romania were, for the most part, a superstitious bunch: they believed that the prudent silence that covered their wounded memory was an aid in calling for the supernatural; everyone prayed in secret. Publicly, numerous "historical" incidents of national salvation were recounted at patriotic festivities. "Historical" is in quotes because the salvations thus recounted were part of a shaky narrative that went back as far as the nation's nebulous founding. It is no coincidence that the first post-communist government in Romania (the unelected profiteers of the 1989 uprising) called themselves "The National *Salvation* Front." These "salvation fronts" appeared in the aftermath of almost every communist state collapse at the end of the 20th century, a formula devised by "intellectuals" in the KGB who understood that power in police states rests on silence and superstition, those

would make love. My notebooks testified to this: whosoever looked back at me when I stared at them in seeming abstraction through the smoky haze of the Figaro, saw a mirror, but it didn't reflect them; they saw instead the infinite process of the making, splintering, remaking, expanding, shrinking of my morphing "self." The Figaro was an exciting cafe on a gloriously hip street, as exciting as the carelessly dressed redhead who was drawing in her notebook. Then she saw me looking at her and laughed. I was skinny as a stick and wearing a Salvation Army coat. It was her laughter I was after, her involuntary reaction to the being with the notebook. Unfortunately, all I could do was frown. Yes, myopia, but I couldn't actually talk to her, not in my rudimentary English.

I wanted to tell her how in my early childhood when I woke up in the dark, unable to open my eyes, my mother sleeping next to me turned into a witch made of ice.[11] My German nanny Ilse[12] washed my shut eyelids with

societies' two pillars of stability, and that when one of those pillars (the police) is knocked down, they must appeal to the myth of "salvation," the ultimate superstition. 1989 was still far in the future of the Romania I left behind when I encountered the US Immigration and Naturalization Service. To me, "becoming an American" was not only part of the "internationalist" mindset of my schooling, but the widely advertised utopia of emigrants, so what could an "American" mean? I knew that citizenship conferred certain privileges (a passport), but I was outraged to discover when I applied for citizenship that I had to pledge allegiance to some kind of "national" identity, for the sake of which I was vetted through lost and shrinking folders by the police. At the time when my youthful arrogance thought itself in possession of a wealth of identities, I was sure that my "stories" and refugee status were sufficient proof of belonging. These stories were not just the currency I thought I could buy my redhead drinks with, but also the coin of an immigrant in the land of them. Instead, I had a file (an anagram for "life"), and I was handed a script to prove my loyalty to the state with formulas inimical to my naiveté. (Or just formulas; the bureaucracy had no use for stories.) For the details see *In America's Shoes*.

[11] My friend Dawn-Michelle Baude asks reasonably: "Did you have a fever?" Her question brought back instantly something I had forgotten: I *did* have a fever the *first* time my mother turned into a witch made of ice and I couldn't open my eyes—I must have been three- or four-years-old. That fever-born image of my mother was so powerful that for the many years that she and I slept in the same bed, all the way to the unseemly age of fourteen—I often had the "witch made out of ice" image in my mind, mostly when I got older and tried to wish away the thought of her body next to mine in the dark. The ice witch guarded the cave of the Incest Taboo. So there were really *three* of us in bed. It seems that I had already invented a persona at a very tender age. (Miss Melanie Klein, to the white courtesy phone, please!)

[12] Ilse's two sons had both been killed in the war, after joining the SS. Their portraits hung over her bed in her neat and cold house. See *The Life & Times...* for the story of how I slept in her crisply-made bed and was warmed by the generous darkness between her legs.

chamomile tea before I could open them. It was a while before I could see, and even longer to remember who "I" was. When "I" was back together for the day, I was sent outside. The city had ghosts: I talked with them, made notes, and wrote poems. At night in bed I shattered again. I "reasoned" myself to sleep; I invented stories in which I was the hero, but my triumph consisted in falling asleep. I must have won endless battles in the cause of sleep. I needed a new "me" every morning of my childhood until I went to school. In school, I wasn't sure that I would ever get a "me" solid enough to stand still for instruction. I fidgeted. I couldn't read. I had to repeat first grade because the letters in the book looked meaningless to me. I suffered terribly until the reading bud opened in my brain, and then I could not only read but write. My stepfather sold my dog Nemo and I vowed revenge. I decided that being human was absurd. I think that my early teachers were kind, but I don't remember them. Something erased them from memory: I recreated them from diffuse affects in various memoirs, but I wonder where they really went. When adolescence surged through me I got the idea that my secret magical weapons gave me a superpower: I was a poet. I had been called to practice an art that could color our monochromatic world: I could read in three languages; I understood and could reach through poetic formulas the mythical creatures living in the Carpathian mountains around Sibiu; I could see and hear people's thoughts; I could see through the adults' masks; using all these abilities I could also *do* anything, especially a weird *something else*[13] that, for lack of a better word, I called "poetry." Still, I couldn't bring back Nemo.

My frown communicated all that to her in a single

[13] This "something else" is a hole shaped exactly like myself, or the "like myself" I might imagine at any given moment, then as now. I'm not analyzing here what might account for this keyhole-shaped absence, except to note that it became a positive value when I decided that my "job" as "poet" was to poke holes. I made it a mission to poke holes in: reality, flawlessness, reason, certainty of any kind, and language(s). Making things hol(e)y, now there is a mission. And then I would ask: and what if I made a hole? And the answer: something strange would come out of it, or if nothing did, I'd fill it back up again. Now Sisyphus and Freud, talk amongst yourselves for a while. It is possible also that in "making a hole" I was only unveiling the dark twin of the history buried in the Archives of Amnesia; what came out of these holes were the figures of my murdered kin. There is no technology for digging deeper than that. Beyond the figures of one's erased self there is nothing.

glance rich enough to make her want to draw me in her notebook. I held her gaze. That flash of understanding, my frown continued, is the fire that never goes out, no matter what the (always temporary) circumstances. It is a fire fed by everything: resentments, to be sure, but also by knowing that she and I were an island surrounded by cookie-cutter fakes. Poets like myself are licensed to invent fabulous selves because they could *see*, a power for which we pay dearly, of course, but which is worth the risk just for sailing the monotonous ocean. The whole cookie-cutter world curses and hunts us, but our powers bypass all the polite forms of general self-invention and make models for more colorful types of humans. Subversive and unhealthy I was as I looked at her, my sketchpad beauty, wanting to tell her all this and more. Failing to hold her gaze, I returned to my verse play. I could barely pay for my coffee. I left change to cover my espresso without leaving a tip, and bolted out the door, abandoning on the round marble table the abused Italian poet Renata Pescanti Botti. She must have called after me because I heard a strangled sound as I ran: I hoped it was the sketch artist, I feared that it was an outraged waiter, but it was probably Renata herself, wounded for being abandoned.[14]

I can't say that the loss of Renata's book pained me greatly. The book had become an *objet* inside which Renata's poems, my drawings and scribbles fused into a single thing. I couldn't have separated them: this book-notebook was a bridge between the fading of calligraphic old Europe and the huge typewriter that was New York. Unlike my first lost notebook, which was

---

[14] Which was the subject of her poems.

the archive of my waking mind, the Renata book was a mongrel thing: nostalgic in places, sore and tender in others, desperate above all to make a multi-lingual escape. I wasn't even sure, as I desecrated the Italian's lyrics, if I was going to write in French, Italian or English: I wrote mellifluous Italian that bugged me with its musicality, honest French that would never be as good as that of Tzara, Fondane, Voronca, Ionesco or Cioran (all Romanian-born second-language French writers) and very primitive English, a language I didn't know and whose poets I was ignorant of. My eventual disposition to one literature or another depended on where I might land a visa. I wanted to come to the US and write in English because both the music (Bob Dylan) and the advice of a respected Romanian poet (Nichita Stănescu) pointed me to English as the future's lingua franca. English ended up suiting me for reasons I figured out only much later, the chief one being that my first language had been German, and a kinship must have formed between my preschool German and my future English. Renata Pescanti Botti's book was my early immigrant workshop: I wrote in it that I discovered an underground tunnel between languages, and said that I could travel it at great speed. I *had* discovered it, but lost the memory of ingress and egress almost immediately.[15]

As soon as I could afford it (by selling single cigarettes in Naples) I bought a

[15] The short "tunnel" between my spoken German (a medieval form of Hochdeutsch) and English was Saxon. The long tunnel was something more mysterious: I think that writing through and over Botti's printed lines in 1965 I was extending my handwriting into print without the intermediary technology of the typewriter. I leapt over the typeset poetry that may have been originally written on a typewriter, the way two decades later post-revolutionary Romanian youth leapt over landlines to cellphones. There was a two to three years' waiting list for landlines when cellphones came into use. At first, the cellphones communicated only one way: Romania was the world's greatest market for fake cellphones in 1991-1993; they were an accessory, a way to pretend-communicate with the world they eventually did communicate with when real cellphones became affordable. The interim was glorious, the young rehearsed their conversation with the "West," without the annoyances of interruption by the other party. When the conversation with the imaginary Western "other" turned from monologue into dialogue, the quality of the discussion diminished considerably. Compromises had to be made: the "other" was not what they imagined—to the detriment of all. My 1965 "tunnel between languages" was also a leap, but of a different technology, a linguistic mental mechanism obvious only to schizophrenics: I boarded my language-train at infantile German, made a stop in French and Italian (via my Belgian friend Marcel in Rome), toured Latin linguistics with Marcel for a good while, before I emerged in 1967 at Penn Station in American English.

blank notebook. Now, besides writing around and over Renata's verses, I composed a long poem on pristine paper in Italian called *Poems from the River Aurelia*, an epic poem-story that described two worlds: a magical underground garden inhabited by women only, and a brutal solar world on the earth's surface where only men lived and waged endless war. Whatever sources in my own psychology this story had were unimportant because I didn't know men.[16] I was raised by a single mother[17] who told me that my father was a beast. A minotaur, I thought. I was the child of a minotaur and a printer. In school, we read Homer and the Greek myths, and every beast was my father: the Minotaur, the Cyclops and even the eye-patched sailors

---

[16] Could Freud have invented a psychology without fathers?

[17] The stepfather I hated was an interlude that I don't consider in any way "paternal," but more like an accident, an unfortunate encounter with a bully on a schoolyard, or the unexpected meeting with the high school soccer player who liked to beat me up (until I hired a bodyguard) because I wore glasses. The Mosesy Pater of Freud didn't exist in my life: that figure was a literary trope I sometimes made use of in my work when "it needed something there," like the painters say. There is one incident within the stepfather accident that might be worth mentioning: the stepfather built a wooden mailbox. I was in a conciliatory mood for some reason (this was before he sold Nemo) and I thought that I might help him, so I wrote in my best childish script with a paintbrush dipped in ink, the words "Mail Box" on the unfinished wood. When my stepfather came home from work, he became livid with rage. He screamed that I had defaced his "mail box," and that I must be punished: he procured some green saplings, threw me on the bed, pulled down my pants and whipped me until his hand tired. I cried despite my stoic intentions, and conceived a hatred of him that achieved its apogee with the sale of Nemo. I can easily construe this freudishly by seeing his anger at my "defacing" of his "male box" as a form of castration that took my mother away from him by making me the more potent male, the "writer," as opposed to "the carpenter." A clear class distinction separated these occupations in the forgotten Austro-Hungarian province we still lived in: "writer" was a "higher" occupation than "carpenter." My childish writing was not deliberately clumsy—I did my best to write straight—but he thought it a deliberate insult to his "male" box. My mother, who was the real "mail box," made only a weak effort to defend me from the whipping. I have had an obsession with mail-boxes, the post office, and postal employees my whole life: I suspect them of evil intentions. They steal my mail, they open it, they use it to read my mind, they sell it to my enemies, etc. Rational arguments as to occasionally lost mail do not allay my sudden bursts of anger. There is "purpose" not "reason" in messing with my "mail" (male). But that's how far the patriarchal influence goes: the "mailbox stepfather" produced one neurosis, not hundreds, like a real father might have. The maternal "river of life" flowed around this jagged rock without great difficulty.

who tied Ulysses to the mast to keep him from loving the Syrens. In Rome I stole Freud's *Die Traumdeutung* (*The Interpretation of Dreams*) and *Zur Psychopathologie des Alltagslebens* (*The Psychopathology of Everyday Life*), and I conducted a painful self-analysis before concluding that all possible complexes were curable by means of metaphor. I was in the right profession. I made a list of "healing metaphors"[18], and they did the job, patching all the holes I needed patched. I stopped the bleeding. What mattered more than my hastily bandaged wounds was magic. The River Aurelia kept flowing, it had to be kept flowing. This wasn't yet a poetics, but an obscure imperative: poetry, if it was to have any value, had to make sure that the river of life kept flowing.[19]

[18] Available on request. The aforementioned books by Freud did not contain the tools for a proper "Freudian analysis," but they provided the tools for a healing through literature. The titles alone were a comfort: I was confirmed in my belief that every daily occurrence had meaning and that it was sick from *something*, a pathology that was my lot to describe and confront, and I felt reaffirmed also for paying attention to my dreams, not only for what they contained, but for what they meant, and for the range of their influence, which extended to the daily. *La vida es sueño*, indeed, a phrase that before Lope de la Vega must have at some point passed the lips of every mortal. One can trace (and this "one" is not me) the beginning of literacy to whomever it was first wrote this down, whether Lope de la Vega or some cabbalist. Most importantly, I discovered that I could summon the feeling of the dream, the *sensation* that life is a dream, whenever faced by a bureaucratic difficulty, or even by pain. These were crude self-devised tools, and they were practical, not intended, as in a proper analysis, to make the unconscious conscious, but inversely, to immerse the conscious into the unconscious, where it could be dealt with by my magical powers. This was a "counter-analysis" of sorts, suggested by Freud himself, who may have covered up his real "cure" with the language of a proper Victorian "profession," in order to please the Father. If he'd been lucky enough, like me, not to have one, we might all be poets now.

[19] I'm writing this sitting on a log on a sandy shore of the Buffalo River. Laura and I are floating from Rush Landing to the White River in a canoe. We set up our tent in a spot hidden by verbena, castor beans, datura, cocklebur, and deadly nightshade. It is the evening of October 3d, 2011 and large death's head moths are feeding on the nightshade trumpets that have just opened. Our driftwood fire is burning, the first stars are out, there is a tall bluff across the river, we can see the white limestone. I hear a coyote. Earlier we saw deer, bobcat, rabbit, raccoon, snake and possibly bear prints in the sand. There are Persephone witches everywhere. Laura is cooking on the fire. There is no phone reception here, so my eighty-six year old mother cannot reach me with her life-long plaint of bad luck, now doubled by physical pain, and fear of death. In this idyll of beautiful and deadly plants, nature doesn't need a telephone, it communicates its menace and beauty without translation. Not me: I take photographs on my iPhone and type this for poetic backup. When reception returns I will email these words and pictures to myself. This iPhone will one day nest in a box of my stuff at Hill Memorial Library. (There will be a longer discussion of digital archiving later, but I note here that my librarian friend, Elaine Smyth, warned me that the pixilated dust in this iPhone may in fact be more ephemeral than any writing on paper. I'll quote Elaine's exact words when I argue against this particular archival fear. Now I will eat.)

Losing the Renata Pescanti Botti's book-notebook was no more painful than losing my watch, which marked and measured, but didn't either store or speed up time. I had mostly abandoned the Renata notebook at about the time that I lost the prized black Pobeda wristwatch my mother gave me when I was thirteen, to mark my passage to manhood.[20] In 1965 in Rome I was, for two weeks, the sex prisoner of two Somalian princesses who kept me from running away from their house by holding my watch for ransom.[21] At that time, the watch must have still stored enough memories to tether me. On the other hand, I cared enough for my dreamy position in that princely household to feign feeling weaker than I actually did. By 1965 the watch ticked pretty faintly

[20] Sleeping in the same bed with my mother one year past the watch-certified age of my manhood was another forgotten (now remembered) war. The "witch made of ice" worked extra hard in that extra year. She melted numerous times and had to be refrozen, like an ice-sculpture that was the centerpiece at a surreal celebration in some oedipal stage set. The watch itself was a Soviet-made time-piece ("Pobeda" means "Victory" in Russian), distinguished by its black screen. To me, Pobeda's black screen was incredibly stylish and represented refusal in its purest form. All wrist-watch faces I had ever seen were white, acquiescing unquestionably to the status quo of our warped society. I could hardly believe that Soviet ideologues, so careful in even the most minute aspects of their structure, would allow for the existence of a black-faced watch, and one named "victory" no less. It was a crack between worlds: the idea that a black watch could claim "victory" was way more than ironic: it was subversive. Time, of all things, had escaped the censors. Either that, or it was a message in a bottle. I got it. Doubtlessly, masses of other people had gotten it: the black Pobeda was a sought-after object, expensive, and nearly impossible to find. It may have been a subversive edition, shipped out before the censors noticed. And they must have noticed: no others were ever made. My Pobeda practically waved the anarchist flag in a sea of red flags. In retrospect, it was fate. "Black" came to mean total resistance to me, a big NO! The "black" of my man-marker watch slipped from its origin in time into all sorts of subsequent symbolic settings. The loss of the watch itself was no more significant in 1970 than the loss of the Renata book-notebook: both had become mere objects after spending their symbolic charge. The watch and the Botti notebook were information-holding devices charged with personal symbols of passage; once the passage (the transition) was made, the things that had held them melted away. Dali's melting clock and Renata's book calling in vain after me were the snake-skins my newborn reptiles left behind.

[21] *The Life & Times of An Involuntary Genius*

already. When it was gone, I felt worse about lying to my mother about what happened to it than having lost it.[22] By the end of the Sixties I no longer cared for either the watch or the language(s) of my birth. The loss of the watch, and finally that of the notebook, meant that I was really free: I was reborn in America without the weight of time on my wrist or the critical frowns of languages my poetry would no longer use.

[22] In this context it's worth telling a story: one late night in Rome I was coming home slightly drunk from Pepino's, a restaurant near the Spanish steps, where I hung out with a motley crew of bohemians. I was accosted by a man in a suit who showed me two glittering gold pocket watches. He told me that he worked at Fiumicino Airport and that he had stolen the two Swiss watches from a tourist's luggage and was now returning to work and had to sell them in a hurry. He showed me the Swiss markings and the 24-carat stamp on the lids and made me listen to their melodious sound. He was so desperate, he said, he was willing to let them go for six hundred thousand lire ($100) if I had it. I didn't have it, but my mother, who kept all our money in a drawer by the bedside table in our room, had just about $100 there, our monthly allowance. I took the watch seller to our apartment building (an hour's walk, which he didn't mind, for all the urgency of his returning to work) and I made him wait outside while I tiptoed past my sleeping mother, slid our cash out the door, slinked out, and bought the watches. I snuck back in again and set the marvelously chiming gold timepieces on the bedside table. I couldn't wait for my mother to wake up to the wonder at their ticking, happy in advance at seeing her delight at my investment savvy. She did indeed wonder at the gold marvels when she woke up, only they had stopped ticking by then. Even so, I showed her the gold-stamp Swiss markings, and she was indeed hugely thrilled. For a full five minutes we possessed a fortune. When we alerted one of our hallway neighbors as to how we had made a killing, he opened the cases and found that the watches had no mechanisms inside, only springs that chimed for the time it took to sell them. It appears that I had been swindled, a possibility we were unwilling to entertain because: 1) we were in the wonderful West we had dreamt about for so long and where only good things happened, and 2) there were the Swiss markings and the gold carat stamps. When we had to accept the truth, we did so reluctantly and provisionally. Both my mother and I believed that the transformation the gold watches had undergone overnight was temporary: the watches would soon return to their ideal, pure gold form. Meanwhile, we had no money. We borrowed some. In my heart of hearts I believed that I had been cheated, but instead of assigning the blame to my emigrant naiveté, I chose to believe that the fraud had to do with the nature of time. My reasoning went something like this: the value of time had been so debased in the country I came from, it fled from contact with us in order to keep its Western (golden) value. The fault rested entirely with the time-killing waste of the bureaucratic swamp we had escaped from, whose malignant odor we still carried with us. When we were going to become American, this odor would disperse, and time would assume its rightful value. My mother never questioned the swindle: she assumed only that it was her bad luck that her son was a bad businessman; if she had handled the transaction, it would have been successful. For the rest of her life, she believed that a lucky break was inevitable: she played the lottery, gambled, bought fakes, made bad investments, was taken at every turn by any glittering offer; every time she lost she blamed the daemon called Luck. This Daemon lived in me, a child she had seen into manhood with the gift of a black-faced Soviet watch. The son-man-daemon had lost his timekeeping marker and thus became an obstacle to Luck. She may have never consciously formulated this thought, but in her search for the source of her bad Luck she must have rested often on this figure. Her father, my grandfather, was killed in the woods with an iron axe by antisemitic bandits; he owned a gold mine and was set upon on a forest path. My mother

*"My Mother's Time"*

was ten-years-old at the time, her father's favorite, and the first man to tell her a lie: he told her that she was a princess and that she would live forever. When no one believed her, she placed her hopes in making a son who would. Alas. Her son didn't, but she never stopped trying. Her father could not have lied, so her son (and all men) who did not believe her father must have been liars (iron axes splitting open her father's truthful skull). She tolerated only men who bought the fairy tale, whether they lied or not, so in her world there was no fake gold. All was either gold or nothing at all. The alchemy of turning the world's lies to gold was only a matter of time. In her mid-eighties my mother gave me a sack full of her wrist-watches, from her earliest delicate piece, to her large, solid time-keeper she wore to work at her printing job, some thirty watches in all styles, from different periods of her life. In 2010 I made a collage-sculpture from an old desk drawer inside which I taped pictures and letters from my mother; I affixed her watches inside the drawer's cubicles. Here is the piece, called "My Mother's Time." Notice that when she is taking the little bundle that is me, home from the hospital where she gave birth, she is wearing a wrist-watch.

Ah, but life is funny. In 2007 I received an e-mail from David Faulds, the rare book librarian at Emory University, inquiring about a poetry book that was part of a donation of poetry books to the library. Inside this book, containing printed Italian poems, a hand had drawn and written what looked like verse in a language that resembled Italian, but wasn't. Is it possible, David Faulds asked, that this book and the handwriting in it belonged to me, the only Romanian poet known to him at the time? David posted a copy from (M)Emory, and yes, indeed, my long-ago act of criminal desecration of Renata's poesy had come to light, more than three decades later. I sent a copy to a poet friend in Romania, Ruxandra Cesereanu, who liked the poems I'd scribbled there in Romanian. She made a copy and sent it to her friend, poet and Vinea Press publisher Nicolae Tzone. A correspondence followed between David Faulds[23], the Romanians, and myself, and this led very quickly, within four months, to a beautiful book containing both a printed transcription of my poems and a facsimile of the entire Renata Pescanti Botti book-notebook. At the time of this publication by Editura Vinea in 2007 I was known in Romania... only in translation. After the fall of the Ceauşescu regime in 1989, my books were being translated from English into Romanian, mostly by the terrific translator and journalist Ioana Avădani, at the rate of two books a year. But now, this book, issued by Vinea, entitled *Femeia neagră a unui culcuş de hoţi* (approx. *The Black Woman in a Thieves' Den*) was not translated; it was in fact my last writing in the Romanian language. Thus in the selva oscura in the middle of mia vita, I found myself at the pivotal center between my first and my second poetry languages. And pivotal it was, because I

[23] A Fauld in time (or fold).

32

felt, like Galileo, that I was orbiting my poetry and had come the closest, nearly four decades later, to the point where my road forked. This was interesting to me (and complicated for others).[24]

[24] A volume of my poetry in Romanian, *Instrumentul Negru* (*The Black Instrument*), appeared in 2005 from the Craiova publisher Scrisul Românesc (Florea Firan, editor). In 1970 I found a folder, typed and with page numbers, for what I must have thought was going to be a book of my last poems in Romanian. The selection must have been made, typed, and paginated around 1968. And then I forgot all about it as I migrated from Detroit to New York and then to San Francisco. When I rediscovered it I sent it to Ştefan Baciu, an exiled Romanian poet who published an expatriate journal in Hawaii, called *Mélé*. Baciu suggested that he would further edit this manuscript by removing a few poems, and offered to write an introduction, and publish it. Baciu was a poet with a considerable reputation in the pre-war era, and a generous supporter of exile literature. He did just that: he made a selection of my selection and wrote an introduction, but he never published it. I once again forgot all about it. Years later, after the 1989 revolution, I unearthed Baciu's selection and showed it to my friend, poet Carmen Firan, who forwarded a copy to her father, the editor at Scrisul Românesc. The book was published in 2005, exactly as Baciu had selected it, with his introduction. In 2007 when Nicolae Tzone issued the facsimile and transcription of the Renata Pescanti Botti book, under the title *Femeia Neagră a unui Culcus de Hoți* (*Black Woman in a Thieves' Den*), we discovered (after the release) that quite a few of the Botti notebook poems were identical to some of the poems in *Instrumentul Negru*. This involuntary overlap was due to my negligence in checking one manuscript against the other, and forgetting that I'd copied at some point some of the poems from the Botti book. I apparently forgot more in the two years between 2005 and 2007 than I forgot between 1970 and 2005. To put it another way, in two years at the start of the 21st century I forgot more than I forgot in fifteen years of the 20th. The first five years of the 21st century seem eight times more eventful than the last fifteen of the 20th, but its events could not have been the cause. The 2007 Giant of Amnesia, only two years old, dove into a pool of my brain, ejecting violently the Nymph of Leisurely Forgetting who splashed there for all fifteen of her years. On discovering the overlap between the two books, Nicolae Tzone became quite angry, though the 2007 book was entirely different, conceptually and content-wise than the 2005 book. In addition to a few of the same poems, the two books had in common only the word "black" in the masculine form of the word in the 2005 title and the feminine form in 2007. (In Romanian nouns are gendered, and adjectives are gendered by the nouns.) The original title of the Botti book-notebook, *Femeia neagră a unui culcuş de hoți* (in facsimile reproduction in the Tzone edition) used the feminine form "black woman" (*femeia* **neagră**), while the later, 1970 Baciu-edited book *The Black Instrument* (*instrumentul* **negru**) used the adjective in its masculine form. Nobody in Romania asked me what or who "the black woman in a thieves' den" was, but many people asked what "the black instrument" might be, reading something vaguely political in the "instrument," but taking it for granted that the "black woman" belonged in the thieves' den. (This may be an unconscious commonplace prejudice/memory of Gipsy harlot-slaves in 19th-century Romanian literature, or a more recent assumption derived from the *1001 Nights*). I decided to say that the "black instrument" was my penis, which made "the black woman" and the original book, subject to it. The original Botti book was then different also in the sense that the unformed young writer felt safe in the skin of a woman hiding in a "thieves den," while the later came out full of machismo to answer questions from the room. The "black instrument" pointed aggressively at Codrescu's fearful old self at just about the time that he became "Codrescu." Some of the poems may have *looked* the same, but they were written by different people: the "black woman" was still Romanian, but the dickhead was "American." (I could have just as easily said that the "black instrument" was the pen, or a gun, but

the question was provocative, and it made me angry enough to invent the truth.) Inspired by the provocation, I made a "return" to the Romanian language, which involved nothing more nor less than recovering what I had been forgetting for thirty-seven years: how to speak and write poetry in Romanian. Stimulated by the discussion around the publication of the two books, I launched into a poetic collaboration by email with Ruxandra Cesereanu, a poet from Cluj. At first, it was an exchange of letters, but as it proceeded it started to change into a poem. The epic result was *Submarinul Iertat*, Ruxandra's title, published in Romania in 2007 by Editura Brumar in a beautiful edition with paintings by Radu Chio and an introduction by Mircea Cărtărescu. I translated this into English as *The Forgiven Submarine* and it was published by Black Widow Press in 2009. (Another "**black**!" And a *widow*, no less. No wonder my favorite song is still The Rolling Stones' "Paint It Black.") Now note the time compression here: one year, 2007, saw both the publication of the original, unadulterated version of my *last* poems in Romanian, and my *first* poetry-writing *and* publication in Romanian, after thirty-seven years of writing no poetry *at all* in Romanian! Thus, the quantity of forgetting between 1970-2007 was equal to the quantity of remembering in five months of 2007 alone. The five-months-old 2007 Giant of Memory was thirty-six-and-a-half times bigger than the Giant of Amnesia! That the Giant of Memory is a lot bigger than the Giant of Amnesia seems to go against common sense: the huge age difference between them raises questions (and eyebrows): did the fifteen-year-old Nymph of the First Forgetting wreak revenge on the Giant of Amnesia, returning from wherever she had been exile-splashed to bring back the substance of memory that she had erased by her leisurely swim in the pool of my time? Where did my Romanian poetry go for thirty-seven years? Even if the Nymph had erased her with vigorous and rhythmic strokes of her tail, the answer has to be that it was lost, just like my first notebook. But unlike my first notebook, I found my poetry language again thirty-seven years later. (Can the notebook be far behind?) The language itself, in its prosaic form, had nearly vanished by 1989 when I returned to Romania as a reporter. I spoke with stones in my mouth: my face and body had taken on the physiognomy of an American-language user; it took several trips to Romania for the rusty machinery of my pedestrian Romanian to start purring again. And then, it was far from poetry; it served mainly to employ a poor repertoire of daily navigation. *The Forgiven Submarine* is an odd title, and much of the poem is trying to elucidate it; I suspect that Ruxandra, consciously or unconsciously, thought of the Romanian language as my "submarine" and, in a gracious gesture, granted me forgiving rights. Someone less generous might have called it *The Forgetting Submarine*, meaning that the language of my childhood and early youth had been submerged like a submarine captained by an incompetent. Given the political rejection of my person in the communist period, Ruxandra was right: if anyone was going to forgive anyone it had to be me. On the other hand, what did "forgiving" have to do with it? This Christian notion issued from Ruxandra, a believing Christian. When we ended (sadly) our poem, its beauty and differences were striking: what I had written was occasionally quite beautiful. I thought of myself as one of those trauma cases where a conk in the head causes the conkee (a lounge piano player) to write Mozart symphonies. I decided to translate the poem into English, mainly to see if I could understand something about the process. The hardest part was translating my own Romanian from the poem into English; Ruxandra's wasn't as vexing. My own "recovered" language was another matter: In Romanian I wrote joyfully, like a kid, delighting in the freshness of the forgotten language-submarine; the poem resurrected forgotten incidents from my childhood, the cloud of smoke around the photographer Nagy who always had a camera around his neck and a joke and a cigarette on his lips, the smell of strudel in Sibiu on Sunday, the whole texture of a time when I was unhappy but magical. Writing the poem gave my childhood memories a retrospectively delightful spin, erasing the nightmares that had actually infused it; I heard the word-music that was the background to my sexual awakening, and first love(s), without the painful struggles that only my lost notebook might testify to; I remembered also my first marshalling of magical defenses against the world. Translating back this excitement into English, the language of my, so to speak, adulthood, proved daunting: to the innocence of words once used in sweet ignorance, to which were now added the wise-obscene meanings that experience feeds expression. Literally the translation works, but in many ways the English version is a new poem. Ruxandra and I toured Romania reading from our collaboration, and we had attentive and stunned audiences; attentive because I was their "lost" poet, stunned because the clashing world-views between Ruxandra and myself signified to the Romanian audience a three-decade literary/theoretical gap between my "free West" and their censored "East." The dimensions of this impression of the "gap" played a role in our reception, but in truth neither Ruxandra nor I, despite our polemically intellectual best-foot-forward, represented any-

Aside from its value to me, Renata's book-notebook was a good example of what is now called "book art," an early experiment with erasure, rewriting, mistranslation and drawing. It seems that in traveling through my language tunnel across Renata's poetry, I was reinventing the wheel of modernism, which had done the same thing for most of the 20th century. The zeitgeist had me doing this on my own, tracing the well-known path of exiled modernists like my dear dadaist Tristan Tzara who scribbled, drew and desecrated most Western writing and art. In the mid-Sixties the dada attack on the well-behaved book of Western civ was de facto. Rebel youth graffitoed every wall. I certainly didn't suffer. I felt that America in the mid-Sixties was a huge book full of well-behaved verses being vandalized by outraged bohemians. I rejoiced. My textual games made me an instantly welcome member of my generation. I felt no loss, only an increase, I was an ongoing hyphen. When I return to Romania now, I am often asked if I am a

thing as universally significant. It's true that Romanian poets had remained focused (if not "frozen") on their own modernist attempts to flee the political demands of "socialist realism," but they hadn't missed much as far as "Western" poetry goes. My part of the poem was a sentimental exercise in pedagogy, an effort to bring Ruxandra's "oneirism" down to earth; her "oneirism" consisted of weird and fabulous metaphors that met my American journalist-first pose. But our **common** belief was that life is but a dream. I was as "oneirist" as she was. Dreams were the engine of my poetry as well as hers, but I, by dint of being "older" and an "American," abrogated to myself extra roles as observer of "hard reality" and "homme du monde." Ruxandra opposed these personae with her own poet-personae, although she herself is also a journalist and a "hard reality" essayist who wrote well-documented pieces on the subject of Romania's communist Gulag. Our poem tried, in a sense, to restore both of our innocences: mine as a Romanian poet, hers as a worthy adversary of prose. But we were both from the field of dreams and from planet Earth. I'm not sure who got the most out of this poetic exercise, but the translation was hard. Still, it was a small price to pay for returning to my native country in the language of my birth. The "lost notebook," if ever found, will belie my ecstatic remembering in *The Forgiven Submarine.* Archivally speaking, the lost notebook contains the child's experience, seen through his own eyes while it was happening, while *The Forgiven Submarine* contains the recovered (and cleansed) memories. And if that's the case, forgetting is indeed a healer performing a magical operation. When the Archives of Amnesia meet the Archives of Remembrance I'll be there, dressed to the nines, with the Nymph of Forgetting dripping wet on my arm. At the piano, Mozart.

Romanian or an American poet, and I usually say that I'm an Amero-Romanian-New Yorker-New Orleanian person who is none of the above, just a poet. My spiritual real estate is vast and nonspecific, I am the archive of everything I've known and everywhere I've been, as Walt Whitman might have put it.[25] The simple-minded impulse to ask that question is unconsciously resentful, but it rests on the belief that leaving one's home without the hope of return represents an irremediable loss. Exiles were to be pitied, like Ovid, who died among strangers and was forgotten in Rome. Ironically, he was exiled to Romania and adopted by Romanians as their first poet. With misguided reciprocity, Romanian poets have been exiled by tyrants ever since. And when tyrants were (rarely) absent, Romanian poets exiled themselves. Those who stayed in Romania found the exiles' condition sorrowful, they imagined them dying from nostalgia. This is pure schlock because nostalgia is not tragedy, and one doesn't die from it. Nonetheless, natives (with help from the state) built a catapult of guilt from their oedipal imaging of the exiles' "longing" for the mother-language and their "betrayal" of the fatherland. The nation-state used this guilt as a unit of currency. It also mined the frontiers, just to make sure. Leaving Romania was forbidden, except for those rare moments when the Iron Curtain parted to let through people like myself and my mother who were bought for hard cash.[26] For every nostalgic, "lost," sentimental soul exported from the nest, the abandoned

[25] Interestingly enough, I googled the word "archive" in my last three books—*The Posthuman Dada Guide: Tzara and Lenin Play Chess* (Princeton University Press, 2009), *The Poetry Lesson* (2010) and *whatever gets you through the night: a story of sheherezade and the arabian entertainments* and I found the word only **once!** in *The Posthuman Dada Guide*, the most researched of the three books, in the following entry:

**Lenin**: *On most new book covers of new biographies from "recently opened" Soviet archives, Lenin looks like a bald eagle photographed by Marion Ettlinger, reflected in Monsieur Tzara's monocle. We derive from this observation, 1) the necessity of being photographed by Marion Ettlinger in order to make a stylish writerly impression, and 2) the reflections of what we will look like in the future will depend on "newly opened archives," even if we are not Lenin. There is a bit of Lenin in all of us, as the reader of a screenplay for this book will doubtlessly tell his Hollywood agent. We will rely on opening archives we didn't know we had.*

[26] Romania's communist dictator, Nicolae Ceaușescu, sold Jews to Israel and Germans to West Germany for hard currency. Israel bought my and my mother's freedom for $4,000 each. The story of this deal is documented in *The Ransom of the Jews: The Story of an Extraordinary Secret Bargain Between Romania and Israel* by Radu Ioanid, preface by Elie Wiesel (Ivan R. Dee, 2005). The story of my coming to the US instead of Israel is told in my book, *The Hole in the Flag: an Exile's Story of Return and Revolution* (William Morrow, 1991).

ethos propagated itself outside its borders; "patrio-
tism" was a manufactured piece of sentiment that was
in reality a valuable means for a small country to export the national ethos; it was certainly more valuable
than what the exiles might have produced had they
stayed. Romanians of the communist era were not very
productive, and their labor, though hard, was worth
next to nothing. The going saw was, "We pretend to
work and they pretend to pay us." Outside the country's borders, exiles woke up as if from heavy slumber
and did well. Each exile didn't earn one million dollars,
but discounted for export to between ten and fifteen
thousand dollars, he or she produced at least ten times
their sale price. The hard cash we were sold for went
into the dictator's secret accounts, while the dollars of
exiles went on to spread the national "ethos" on every
continent. The only "hard" nostalgia of exiles was for
their childhood, which is irretrievable no matter where
one lives. Childhood is lost in time, not in language
or space. I speak for others here, because I have little
nostalgia for mine. I had nothing to contribute to the
state I left behind, but, as it turned out, I gave Romania
a good rep in America anyway, just by mentioning it
often and keeping up with its fortunes. Nostalgia ad-
vances the interests of states and tribes, but if it exists at all outside of the longing for the "paradise of
childhood," it is outweighed by a great joy that goes
mostly unacknowledged. The exiled condition is sin-
fully fertile. When, additionally, the zeitgeist meets this
unspoken pleasure, as it did for me, it fills the expat's
notebooks with the ejaculate of numberless personae.
I simply couldn't keep all those selves to myself. I had
escaped with an imagination[27] full of people, and I was
ready to give them to you, redheaded girl with drawing

[27] Imagination is masturbation: the
projection (doubling) of self into a
fuzzy medium, a virtual world. There
are a finite number of such worlds,
a long stutter. I will reprise this in a
later footnote.

pad who may or may not have called after me at Cafe Figaro, corner of Bleecker and MacDougal.

Renata Pescanti Botti's refound book brought back the memory of my first notebook (the *truly* lost one), it returned to me my first history, the specific ambitions of poetry in that long-ago time. That first notebook, to continue with the geometrical metaphor, was the beginning of my orbit, the start of my moving around the fixed center of poetry. When I deliberately abandoned the lined notebook something in me erased borders, it blurred the boundary between the austro-hungro-calligraphic border of my schooling and the soviet border I ironically crossed to get the unlined notebook.[28] In the decades that had elapsed, the Renata *objet* had not moved with me; it had no history, it had been *lost*. But now that it was found and published, my journey in English pointed me back to my start in Romanian. I remembered *why* I started writing, and felt just like the virgin I was until Marinella and M.R. Paraschivescu relieved me of it—Marinella of my physical one, the poet Paraschivescu of my publishing one.[29] I wanted to be "between the covers," in books and in the flesh. If the *why* looked at first like gaining significance to extract revenge and gain solace, it soon added something else: making words change the whole existing world[30], a project that was proper to poetry, especially in the mid-20th century when political ideologies, East and West, were losing credibility. Poetry translated as anarchism, though it kept, in my view, a transcendental reserve, a store of otherworldliness that the music of the day told us would be the sound of heaven. What gave a poem such disproportionate weight, compared to much longer texts, was that it had to be smart[31],

[28] This is multi-layered irony: the rigid calligraphy we were taught was a relic of the old empire, a slanted, German-style hand; the Soviets attempted to change the writing of Romanian from Latin characters to Slavonic ones, an effort that failed, but that retained in filigree the freedom of the exploded verse of constructivist Russian poets, like Majakovski, who had made the unlined (free) page the signature of modernity. The lines may have disappeared because of my daring visit to Kniga Ruskaya, but my handwriting stayed the same, an inner tension lost now but once a rare object: the austro-hungro-calligraphic empire butting up against the soviet tanks of orthographic freedom. A small object really, but an historic monument in its way.

[29] Here may be a fugitive reason for nostalgia: revirginating by means of a lost childhood totem.

[30] While simultaneously poking holes in it. ("Overthrowing" is herculean while "hole poking" is talmudic.)

[31] I originally wrote "unique" instead of smart, but then realized that no poem (or any utterance) could help but be unique; it's the curse (or blessing) of the fingerprint.

and, in order to be so, it had to be implicitly a critique of all the poems that came before it; it had to contain the history of the genre[32] while overthrowing it. It thus required all the knowledge of what it was it was overthrowing, which made it first of all an archive. Take my 1971 "history:"[33]

> *in 1946 there was my mother inside whom*
> *i was still hiding.*
> *in 1953 i was small enough to curl behind a tire*
> *until the man with the knife passed.*
> *in 1953 i also felt comfortable under the table*
> *while everyone cried because stalin was dead.*
> *in 1965 i hid inside my head*
> *and the colors were formidable.*
> *and just now at the end of 1971*
> *i could have hidden inside the comfy hollow*
> *in the phone*
> *but i couldn't find the entrance.*

An autobiographical list, the poem sets out ostensibly to mark my private circumstances within the bigger history of the world. It begins in the moment just before my birth, but unlike, let's say, Tristram Shandy or the jokes about babies refusing to be born if they aren't promised something impossible, I am *hiding*. The womb is a good place and I know that outside of it is hell. The edenic womb and the satanic world are not new ideas, but the prescient inhabitant of Eden is a rare creature. He *remembers* the future. Paradise is a priori amnesic, happiness having no business with either past or future: it is an eternal present. It is absurd to know anything in the womb, where Adam and Eve knew no sin and could not predict it; they could only

---

[32] Note yet another job for poetry.

[33] *The History of the Growth of Heaven* (George Braziller, 1972).

take God at his word that knowledge was bad. Creating a limited term (nine months) replica of Paradise within the woman he had already punished with the pains of birth was a cruel irony. For this inhabitant of the replica who knows that it's all a bad joke, there is a reason to *hide*. He has established the act of hiding as an alternative to history. Of course, he could also die—suicide in the womb is not rare—but then there would be no record. The established myths overthrown by this prenatal discovery are numerous: among them is the myth of the eternal efficacy of God's punishment; the myth of God's irony; the myth of the world itself, ruled by history, but not unopposed. What comes next is war with that world and its history: the man with the knife passed in a dream (a dream I had at about age three or four); it was still possible to hide from him by appealing to that prenatal smallness that had shielded me not long before. That ability to shrink, smuggled from the womb, was the one edenic skill that the infant snuck past the angel with the finger on the lips. I knew how to make myself small, but I still didn't know yet the difference between the dream of the man with the knife and the world where that man could cause real blood to flow. Dream and reality hadn't yet separated; there was still a transparent membrane, a clean window between the inside and the outside. Being able to hide from a dream killer was my earliest triumph in the postnatal world. Stalin's death was a day of national rejoicing for the slaves of his empire, a joy that had to be carefully disguised as mourning. Only a child hidden under the table between the legs of grownups could experience that joy unencumbered. The legs of the grownups could communicate what their upper bodies with the heads could not. I read those legs and was happy. The skill of hiding added to itself the knowledge of reading the truth of the body divided between its lower (and truthful) motions and its higher (and lying) despair of surrender. In 1965 I took LSD in Italy and I saw that I had never left the womb, and that it was possible to be in heaven no matter where I was. In fact, no human had ever left the womb but for being tricked by the story of history. And that story, for the brief time of the psychedelic flight, was reversible. I saw the formidable colors of paradise that people not on LSD preferred to *hide from*. I didn't have to hide from what I saw just because the world hid itself from what I was seeing. The clanging gate of the womb resonated forever in peoples' skulls, causing most humans to simply disbelieve, dismiss paradise as a fiction, and believe God's cruel lie. Thus *hiding* had two manifestations: a personal, survival-driven activity of the threatened child, and the collective fear-driven blindness of the adult world. As my research proceeded, I saw that the formidable colors of paradise had another nemesis: a technological lookalike, a simulacrum of innocence and connection that was also an instrument of incarceration. I could have hidden in the phone (the techno-simulation of 1971, and you can insert here visions of all the instrumental virtualities that came after) but I couldn't "find the entrance." As a seasoned human, I permitted myself a bit of irony: the entrance to the virtual world of telephonic heaven was bigger than a subway entrance and at least as wide as the gate to Buckingham Palace. You had to be either blind or seriously misled to miss it, or just a funny guy who'd rather not. I was a funny guy.[34] Hiding, in all its three forms (childish fear, adult terror and virtual heaven) was unnecessary. The poem lists only a few big moments, but it could have gone on, and it can

[34] A *hardworking* funny guy: poking holes to make hideouts or to reach tunnels is strictly a shovel job, a task for one body and one tool; using any instrument more sophisticated than a muscle-powered shovel complicates things too much, because the digging tool has to be pulled into the hidey hole along with the "self" trying to evanesce. Can't leave clues behind for trackers. The greedy and the overly sophisticated get caught. The world is covered with jewels and abandoned tractors.

still be added to: a lot happened to both of us, me and world, since 1971. It's a list poem and thus archival, but it's actively archival, it is an archival machine that moves through time in time to the imperative of the poet, which is to counter history by demolishing, or at least misdirecting, its archival certainties.[35] What history of poetry (unlike the very public one) I critiqued in my lower case "history" was rudimentary: romanticism, idealism, impressionism, cubism, social realism, etc. Art could not be saved. This conclusion, not quite clear in 1971, drove the list nonetheless. I could have leapt then (in 1971) to the fortune-cookie revolutions of J.P. Sartre or Guy Debord, whose analyses were in no way wrong, but whose prescriptions, in my view, lacked poetry. To *think* so well and to resolve so wrongly (in sloganeering) wasn't what my "history" was willing to accept.[36]

In my adolescence I'd collected books in a glass case: precious, slender volumes by young Romanian poets, printed on bad quality paper and heftier, bound works of the permitted classics. I read my books often and kept them clean and dusted, making sure that all the spines were aligned and visible. I started by ordering them alphabetically, but I later combined them by style or affinity, or even by origin (I had a shelf of poets' *first* books), sometimes by whether they were in translation

[35] Note the addition of "demolition" and "misdirection" to "overthrowing" and "poking holes" in the growing list of attempts at defining poetry. The (possibly) most successful product of this process of essaying a definition for poetry is making several "poetry machines," like the "history" whose footnote this is; the best poetry machines function in the four ways Ted Berrigan told me were necessary to make a poem work: up and down and sideways. (This makes a cross, as I commented several times. "Commenting several times" is itself a poetry machine: if one keeps, as I seem to do, only a few revelatory incidents for poetic use, they must be reprised every time I write, in order to critique them—like the history of poetry—understand them a little more, defend them if I must, or just reinforce them like an old house that needs new supports.) The "poetry machines" go into anonymous production immediately, unlike the "self" with the shovel who plans its disappearance before digging ("poking") a hole. One could, I suppose, invent a poetry-machine that tracks down the fugitive poet, but why help posterity? This is the archivist's job, working with "archive/research" machines.

[36] In this matter I had something to teach my friends: not having experienced marxist rhetoric, socialism with or without a human face, they had no idea that the Ayatollah Khomeini and Pol Pot were just around the corner, a few years hence, waiting to take the lofty view of the killing fields from the aerie of theory down to ground-level.

or in the original. I didn't collect much prose, but I liked reading Jules Verne and Conan Doyle, and later Mark Twain, Sinclair Lewis, John Steinbeck and Farley Mowatt, who were the only English language writers the communists approved of. These prose translations I kept on the lowest shelf in no particular order. I read also an immense quantity of unapproved literature in the form of books borrowed hush-hush and passed on with a look around. Three of these books rocked my world: *Le Mythe de l'éternel retour: Archétypes et répetition* (*The Myth of the Eternal Return: Archetypes and Repetition*) by Mircea Eliade, *Un Précis de decomposition* (*A Manual for Rotting*) by Emil Cioran and *Poemele Luminii* (*Poems of Light*) by Lucian Blaga. Two of them were in French, one in Romanian: all three were forbidden. Owning a copy was a crime. The official reason for their illegality was that they were mystical; mysticism and religion were enemies of dialectical Marxism, therefore these books were enemies of the people. The real reason was that all three authors had been right-wing nationalists, which in the mid-Sixties was still a bad thing. After Ceaușescu came to power he adopted nationalism to go with his marxism, a winning combination that kept him on the throne for nearly four more decades. I learned from Eliade's book that all religions had in common Paradise, the center of the world (Axis Mundi), and the Tree of Life. Life itself was possible because of the memory and practice of one's beliefs in these symbolic places. Religious rituals were performed in imitation of the gods' first acts, which had all taken place at the center of the world under the tree of Eden. During the time of the performance of rituals one was transported from regular, daily time to a time outside of time; a timeless, sacred time.[37] Eliade's

[37] I read his book, *The Sacred and the Profane*, in English, much later, in 1967, when Eliade gave me a copy himself.

philosophy fit my world-view like a wetsuit. I spent at least an hour a day exploring the streets of my medieval town in search of the Axis Mundi and the Tree of Life. I closed my eyes and sometimes banged my head against a stone wall of the Evangelical Cathedral to induce a kind of trance that I called "paradisiacal." I had bumps on my head and I felt high like they said marijuana made you feel in the capitalist West where the jazz musicians smoked it. The Axis Mundi, I decided, was wherever I felt that high, which transported me to Paradise from the dull school and boring apartment I lived in with my mother. Repeating the rituals of my religion was more difficult because I didn't have any. Any official one, that is. I was a secular Jew in a Christian Orthodox world that was officially atheist. I decided that poetry was my religion and that its rituals were as follows: putting up the collar of my school uniform jacket every morning, wearing my kepi backwards, keeping on a look of disdain for this world (sexy, no?), smoking at least two cigarettes a day while hanging out at a coffeehouse near high school as my teachers went by, and writing in my notebook regularly. I also practiced "sacrilege," as noted in my notebook, and I elaborated a prayer that was also an alchemical formula (and which I believed could be used for bad magic against anyone who dared insult my poetry). Like Eliade, I too believed that there were two of everything, one good and one bad: children (good), adults (bad), poetry (good), prose (bad), imagination (good), realism (bad), communism (bad), anarchy (good), and so on until our physics teacher who was Greek told me that every word in ancient Greek contained its opposite, and that those ancient Greeks had either solved or complicated the problem by making all things contain a dual nature. I

said that they were wise to do that, and she said maybe.
I now know that she was familiar with quantum theory,
and that Heraclitus had already brushed aside particle-
wave dualism, not that anybody noticed. I didn't: I was
right there with Eliade and Marx. One kind of time
was profane because it was faithless (or capitalist), and
the other kind was holy because it imitated the gods
(the utopia of the past) or strived for communism (the
utopia of the future). The time we lived in was called
"history," and it was bad, profane, and decayed because
it was godless and not yet communism. This was dialec-
tics and it didn't make living in the present much fun. It
wasn't. Emil Cioran's *Manual for Rotting* took Eliade's
dialectic to greater and more emphatic depths: history
was not only profane, it was the process of human evil
par excellence, eradicable only through the destruction
of humans. We had fallen from Eden into History and
death was our only (otherwise inevitable) salvation. He
recommended suicide. This bleak existentialist vision
was oddly tonic and comic in the vein the French call
"humor noir." To this heady mix was added the visionary utopia of Lucian Blaga's poetry, a paradisiacal world
of pre-Christian bliss ruled by the sex god Pan. Blaga
didn't even concern himself with history; he dwelt already and only in Eden, though he was still alive when
I first read him, working as a librarian and translator but
forbidden to publish original poetry. Scores of young
people found him anyway and met the man who lived
(in his poetry) in Eden. Blaga said that Eden was to
be found in the eternal peasant village—in his words,
"eternity was born in the village"—but he lived in Cluj,
a large city. He too had been exiled from Eden, though
he was geographically close to Lancrăm, his birthplace
and model for Eden.

I met the first of my literary heroes, Mircea Eliade, in 1967, less than a year after I emigrated.[38] It turns out that many of my literary contemporaries, including Allen Ginsberg, had sought out Professor Eliade at the University of Chicago around that time, because his study of shamanism and other visionary religious practices phrased elegantly and concisely what they had seen themselves during psychedelic visions. There certainly was a sacred time, psychedelic time, when the universe came to life with all its illuminated connective tissue. But was there such a thing as "profane" time? Probably not, unless one counted blessed unconsciousness as profane. I now think of it as a holy defense against the exhausting vividness of the living universe, a kind of sleep granted humans, the privilege of stupidity[39], our special reward for seeing so much and being so helpless. Back then I didn't see that the kind of division that privileges the religious over the nonbeliever was the same division that privileges the state over the individual, the army over the civilian, and the aristocrat (or the rich) over the poor. Eliade's work reinforced the schema sketched by Georges Dumézil about the fundamental powers of Western civilization: the King (or the State), the Church, and the Army. I'm on the lookout now for the seductive traps of my generation:

[38] A few months after arriving in the US in 1966, I hitchhiked to Chicago to meet Mircea Eliade. I was received most cordially by the Eliades. I stayed at the YMCA for $3/night, I ate nearly nothing during the day, but I was determined to see Eliade for as long as he cared to see me; this turned out to be ten days, during which I was a thief's assistant, a dishwasher, a pizza delivery boy and, briefly, homeless. But I had my time with my scholar-hero and his brusque, witty and charming wife Cristinel. In the evening they took me to restaurants where I ate rich food, drank wine and talked nonsense. Soon after I took my leave, I vomited everything, including the contents of our conversations, only fragments of which survived in my diary. I hitchhiked back to Detroit very pleased with myself and initiated a correspondence with Eliade that lasted for one year and ended abruptly when I criticized the English translation of his favorite novel, *The Forbidden Forest*, first written in French and published there as *La Forêt Interdite*.

[39] I heard a political candidate say that he was out to "defend our dreams," to which the only rejoinder is, "defend us *from* our dreams." Please. "Dream" is the most dilatory word in the American political vocabulary; telling the mobs what their dreams are is a favorite form of demagoguery, a "dream-reading" in reverse: we'll tell you what your "dreams" are, and then we'll decipher and defend them for you. "Dream" as "wish" defangs the experience every time a pol mouths it. Does "meaning" accrue from subtracting "sense"? The "poetical" (political) does to language what radioactivity does to landscape: it makes it uninhabitable. Since anything can be used "poetically," language must be severely geigered every time it hits the airwaves.

[40] Like a thermometer.

[41] To this day I don't own my favorite books, I always lend them out, never to see them again. Publicizing mystical belief was one of the three features of two simultaneous mystical movements born in Romania in the mid-19th century: hassidism and christian-orthodox monastic ecstatic practice; according to Moshe Idel the other features were prayer and worship of the figure of the saint. Mysticism, until that time and in that particular place, was occult, hidden. The idea of democratizing it occurred when "publicity" ceased to be a shameful word, thanks to the revelation by economists of global markets, and the new-born American art of marketing. (Ideas simultaneously "in the air," not necessarily known even to the locals, literally took to "the air," via newspapers and the radio.) Mystical practice was secret by default; the shedding of its cover in two religions that were officially at odds is even odder for its emergence in an obscure corner of Romania: it testifies to a world already globalized, before the overt connections surfaced. Mystical practices, for all their static appearances (meditation, etc) were in fact conduits of global consciousness, proof perhaps that the experience of divinity is an experience of communality, totality, globality, universality. The shamanic internet was at work long before the technological version.

under the pleasant weather of vaguely conceived spirituality, many of us were providing cover for the conservative antidemocratic forces of the coming decades. Eliade had written on other subjects of interest to my generation, among them yoga and witchcraft. His books, *Yoga: Freedom and Immortality* and *Shamanism: Ancient Techniques of Ecstasy*, achieved scriptural status. Eliade's work confirmed that magic was at the root of all religions, and that the ubiquity of certain sacred symbols suggested that all things were imbued by the divine with life, counter to the artificially divided (by 19th-century science) regnums of animal, plant, mineral, astral and cosmic matter. Eliade himself gave his research into religions a scientific patina. The exalted knowledge available fast (for us young'uns) in a pill or plant, or slowly through spiritual exercises like fasting, meditation, or banging your head on a cathedral wall, made the diurnal world we actually lived in seem like a pathetic virtual reality that had to be either ignored or overthrown. Ignoring it necessitated the dark humor of Cioran (the only existentialist who made you laugh while killing yourself), and, possibly, the sexual ecstasy of living permanently in the "light." These Romanian writers who initiated me made it impossible for the alienated and angry adolescent I was to yearn for anything but the deepest, darkest, and most instrumental poetry. This instrument was the intuitive force I needed to explore the world of the sacred; the instrument itself was writing, it looked like a line of verse.[40] I didn't need to own my masters' dangerous books, not because I was afraid to own them, but because they were meant to be shared. Passing them on to others was a mission.[41] The books I read often provided me with equipment, as if I was preparing to climb

Everest: Rilke donated wings, Arghezi a carving knife, Blaga a sheep skin, Eliade a filigree[42], Cioran a sinister chuckle, Tzara a hat made from a newspaper, and Nina Cassian handed me a seahorse on a window-sill while it snowed in the mountains. I carried these totems everywhere.[43] Actually, any book available for sale or sub rosa in the censor-perforated library of the late 1950s, early 1960s—from Eliade, Cioran, Blaga, Seferis, Tzara or Majakovski—left behind a totem to add to my mental altar. I memorized at least one line from each poet, an object to be placed there. I recommended this use of poetry to my students when I was teaching: it armed them with a theater of *ars memoria*.

Archives librarian Elaine Smyth asked me whether I re-read or annotated my books, beginning with this early library, and the answer is a resounding "yes." I must have either seen or read somewhere an essay about marginalia, so I had no qualms about underlining, writing on the margins, making symbolic marks (one exclamation point for Great, three for Terrific, five for Marvelous and, of course, innumerable single and multiple question marks; the sizes mattered, too: a BIG exclamation point meant GREAT, and so on.) I remember some of my notes as very good and concise pro or con arguments against something or other, but others were unconnected to the passage, being just something that occurred to me in some remote connection. There are embarrassing notes too, that are shown up a few sentences later in the book, the author having predicted my facile objections. Sometimes I copied my notes, especially early on, and I often used both marked passages and notes for some writing in progress. My early notes were in a neat hand because I was self-conscious

[42] A testing kit.

[43] Like the Ice Age man found frozen in the Swiss Alps.

and neat, but I later became quite violent in my response to the text and wrote furiously (and unintelligibly now) things I felt passionate about.[44] A few books I thought of as too valuable to scribble on—beautifully printed books with art or rare volumes I hoped to sell—but there were few of these, and I didn't read them very well. I tried not to mess with poetry books, unless they gave me an idea for a line or so, which happened often. It was (and still is) difficult for me to finish an exciting book: I begin retorting to it from almost the first sentence, and if I do finish it, I end up rewriting it. American books on a shelf give no clue if they have been read or not if there is no marginalia, but French books when I first started seeing them had to have their pages cut while reading, a wonderful gauge of reader interest. I remember visiting Jean-Pierre Faye in Paris and noting with satisfaction, as he poured some drinks in the kitchen, that some major philosophical works on his shelves stopped being cut a few pages in (though the cut ones were amply annotated). I hastily put them back when he returned. It's worth noting in this context that my most heavily annotated books are essays about philosophy and religious/mythical texts. If an archival impulse is present anywhere in my notes, from the very first in the lost notebook to the marginalia, it doesn't have to do with the question, "Does God exist or not?" to which the correct proletarian answer is, "Yes, God does not exist,"[45] but as to whether the Archives is God. Or vice versa. Noah's Arc-Hive is a point in case: when God told Noah about the flood, did He personally order the drunkard to archive a pair of every animal on earth? Or was it Noah's idea, in view of the fact that God desired only to destroy the earth's wicked inhabitants? Noah's Arc-Hive is a collection of

---

[44] I made notes on the margins of thousands of student papers in twenty-five years of teaching; I tried to write concisely in a clear, neat hand that many of them found illegible anyway. My German-learned calligraphy tried to make itself legible to my American students, but my attempts to imitate handwriting taught in the US ended up as a hybrid of lower-case printing (when I was feeling "neutral") and an orthographic shorthand interspersed with European cursive (when I cared). The point of this is that an anthology (or a series of anthologies) of teacher comments on student papers, would make amusing reading. The story could begin in first grade and follow the student through herm doctoral thesis, making a series of slant sub-biographical narratives. Every student/author (who is everyone in the modern world) could present in evidence herm teacher's notes (nicely reproduced and bound in velour) as a critical work on herm writing/thinking, if herm is ever called for a Grand Reference (like in a criminal trial, or before G-D.) Or people could simply exchange these collections of comments for fun or profit. *The Mind of an Era As Seen Through the Comments of My Teachers in the 1970s* is already a best-seller. Amazon, take note.

[45] Alexandr Zinoviev, *The Yawning Heights* (Random House, 1979).

genetic information that assures the survival of life on earth. There is no record of which animals Noah and family made extinct by eating them during the voyage, just as there is no record of which plants no longer exist because hungry scientists ate some of the vast seed collection they hid from the nazis during the siege of Leningrad. There are two Archives, the saved and the consumed, and my notes pursued this idea and the arc of time it spanned (from the mythical to the historical) no matter what the subject at hand. My notes are queries about poetry, the religion of, the stuff it is made from. The notes are questions about present and missing knowledge, but I don't think I ever thought of the notes themselves as archival: they are, after all, only writing on paper, nowhere as complete as the genes of animals and plants. Or maybe not: did not César Vallejo hyperbolically proclaim the poet, "un pequeño dios"?

My first private library displayed only permitted names, it was indeed a collection, clean and cared for. I could have harbored illicit volumes too, because all books were available in one way or another, but my mother was afraid of being discovered with these goods. Out of deference to her (and because I passed them on to my friends) I didn't keep forbidden books. If possible, the state, like the church, would have outlawed all books but for their scriptures, but that was unenforceable, and ignored. When we emigrated I had to leave all my books behind because we were only allowed a small suitcase. Goodbye, my first library! In my brain, however, totemic poetry objects were arrayed in a memorable structure.

When I reached the West, in Napoli, Italy, a Christian

missionary gave me the first book of my new life: a Bible in Romanian, printed beautifully on fine paper. This, my first "free world" book, before acquiring Renata Pescanti Botti's notorious volume, I still have; it sits now in a row of collectible Bibles in various translations, including the Gnostic Bible translated into English by my friend Willis Barnstone. My first job in the US was at the Detroit City Library in 1967. I was equipped with a pair of roller-skates and sent careening through the stacks holding a tube sent from three stories above via a pneumatic device like the mail in 19th-century Paris. It contained a book order. This job lasted only three days because a well-meaning colleague handed me a pleasure-inducing tablet that turned out to be mescaline. By the time I'd rolled about the shelves at great speed on my roller-skates, the letters on book spines became a delightful blur and I was overwhelmed by the range of colors and sentiments they emanated. I'd still be zipping by book spines and considering this the greatest poetic activity if the worried management hadn't sent for the paramedics. They didn't understand that I was a man from the future who "read" through screens installed behind his eyeballs. They didn't understand that content disappears at certain speeds, leaving behind only color and motion, just like style in literature dispenses with content *inside* books. I had become style and a victim of propriety, a bad fate for a nineteen-year-old immigrant. Happily, those were lax days: all they took away were my roller-skates, they didn't confiscate my notebooks. Detroit, on the other hand, went up in flames. Downtown Detroit burned while on the radio Jose Feliciano sang "C'mon baby, light my fire!"

In 1968 in New York I worked part-time at the 8th

Street Bookshop, a writer's bookstore, and I could suddenly have any book I wanted. The Wilentz brothers, owners of the 8th Street Bookshop, were also partners and supporters of now-famous small presses such as Yugen, Jargon Books and Something Else Press. An entire shelf upstairs held every issue of these and other small press publications. I took them all home and mostly forgot to return them. Everyone who was anyone came into the bookstore: Allen Ginsberg, Ted Berrigan, Philip Roth, Norman Mailer, Ronald Sukenick. I had them sign all their books. All my fellow clerks were poets, and we were proud that Gregory Corso and A.B. Spellman had clerked here in the past. Penurious bards from the East Village strolled in and stole books under our benevolent (unless they overdid it) gaze. The two-room-bathtub-in-the-kitchen $60/month apartment on Avenue C[46] was crammed full of poetry books. I prized curiosities, like James Dickey's *Drowning with Others*, collated by mistake within the covers of John Ashbery's *Some Trees*, and signed, unwittingly, by both of them. I owned copy #5 of the signed limited edition of Tom Veitch's mimeographed poetry book *My Father's Golden Eye*. When I told Tom that I didn't know I rated so highly in his eyes as to deserve #5, he said, "Don't worry... They are all number five." The real perk of the 8th Street Bookshop was the occasional hors-commerce conversation with a writer; one afternoon when Anaïs Nin came into the store looking for a magazine and I ended up talking a book's worth with her alone. I arranged the books by writers I'd met on their own shelf.

1968 to 1970 in New York were golden years for absorbing the English language: writing, reading, hanging out with poets, developing firm esthetic prejudices and

[46] Where I lived with Alice, my girlfriend, then my first wife and mother of my two children, Lucian (after Lucian Blaga) and Tristan (after Tristan Tzara).

indulging day and night in stoned collaborations with friends, some of whom became famous and are now dead, and some of whom are just dead. I knew that I was living through an extraordinary period in the arts, and I started, prankishly, to think about the future disposition of my image, even if I didn't think about an Archives, per se. I initiated a correspondence with my friend Michael Stephens, who lived uptown on the West Side: we wrote to each other every day, taking our geographical cues from our locations, me in the East (Lower East Side), he in the West (Upper West Side). Every day I would post a letter from the "East," with an "eastern" address at the top of the page, like "Bangkok, April 12, 1968," and Michael would write back from the "West": "Copenhagen, April 13, 1968." We kept up this correspondence for a couple of months, making sure that our imaginary eastern and western countries were alluded to in great detail, and that the ambiance of the writing evoked those places (Thailand, Denmark) as accurately as we could make them. We stopped only when the confusion between east and west became too great to handle: I was an immigrant from eastern Europe, but the "East" itself was generally understood in the United States to mean "the Orient," so we took this last notion as our cue. On the other hand, we weren't quite sure what was either east or west in global terms, because the earth is round, so we argued about this when we saw each other, until we had to stop corresponding because we couldn't agree. (It was around this time that the philosophical and geographical uncertainty between such notions as "the West," "the East," "the Orient" and "the Occident" began troubling academic scholars as well, but we didn't know it, just as we didn't know that our correspondence was a "postmodern" literary work. We certainly thought of it as a literary work, but "postmodern" wasn't in our vocabulary yet. We had read J.L. Borges' essay about the tenuousness of geographical labels, and maybe it was this essay that put an end to our letters.) This short epistolary novel by Michael Stephens and myself was meant to be taken literally by future researchers, who would see what great adventurers we had been (in addition to being, obviously, great writers). Any look at the envelopes would have, of course, given us away, since they were all posted from New York City. I thought about this at the time, but the hassle of actually finding someone in Bangkok or Copenhagen to mail the letters was too much. I was surprised when, many years later, LSU's Hill Memorial Library went through my stacks of letters, took them out, and returned the envelopes to me! I could hardly believe it. I'm no collector but I know that stamps, dates and envelopes are half the game of collecting. I'll chalk it up to a green intern. I kept the envelopes awhile, then I threw them out, though I felt uneasy: some of the envelopes had drawings, messages and told stories in even their plainest directions. Maybe this decision was not an intern's, but more akin to what many public libraries do, which is to strip the jacket from hardback books and bury them in plastic. There may be budgetary reasons, but destroying the art, the blurbs, the author's picture and bio, and flap jacket information, seems criminal to me. The intern did us a favor: the first scholar who takes our letters literally will have to wonder how we knew the secret of time-travel. In the late Sixties we were, of course, a long time from that: sometimes we drew our "eastern" or "western" stamps by hand, next to the official US ones. In the late

Eighties, just before the revolution that overthrew the communist regime in Poland, artists drew politically subversive stamps by hand on letters they sent to each other, and the Post Office allowed them to go through, allying themselves in this way with the revolution. After the revolution, these handmade stamps and their envelopes became much more valuable than the ones issued officially by the state.

Another experiment of the late Sixties was my one-year "alternative" diary. In the morning I would have coffee and a donut at Blimpie's[47] on 6th Avenue between 9th and 10th Streets, across the way from the Women's Prison, a building since demolished. I tried to get up early enough to watch the Catholic high school girls go by in their uniforms, swinging their school bags, and see the inmates whistle at them through the bars. The donut shop had a big plate glass window and I made sure that I got a good seat. I would then write my "journal" for the day, using some of the passing girls and stationary inmates as characters; I would describe my day in detail, featuring sexy encounters and adding "mundane" occurrences for "authenticity." In the evening of that same day (mostly at work) I would open another notebook and note, more tersely and in less detail, the real occurrences of that day, which were more or less routine. I intended to re-read in "the future," twenty years hence, say, both the imaginary and the real journals, to see if I could tell the difference. I was convinced that I wouldn't be able to. I never tested this assumption because I never re-read those journals side by side, a still-interesting project that I doubt I'll ever undertake. Take note, young researcher!

[47] Blimpie's was everywhere in New York in those days, a precursor of Subway, or maybe an earlier incarnation or competitor of Dunkin Donuts. When New York reinvented itself in the Eighties, it chased America out, and recreated its early 20th-century quasi-European atmosphere. This was good for real estate, but chainstore America came anyway, in the Nineties, because the high-rent neo-natives wanted atmosphere *and* efficiency. Part of the pact with Mall America was the construction of architecturally outlandish apartment buildings that quoted modernism and postmodernism as if the Sixties were still present on some kind of "artistic" continuum. The difference was mere money: the late Sixties $5 bag of groceries became the Nineties $50 gram of cheese. In late 2011 as I write this, the housing slump hasn't hit Manhattan as hard as the suburbs, but there is, no doubt, another metamorphosis on the way. Cheese is heading for $500—the goat giggles.

In addition to these projects with a view to my personal future biographers, I also invented poets. My poets included a jailed Puerto-Rican, a Vietnam vet, and a lesbian protofeminist, who were meant to publish separate books, but ended up abbreviated instead under one cover in my debut collection, *License to Carry a Gun*. In addition, there was Calvin Boone, a Benedictine monk whose poems were issued in mimeograph in 1971 as *The History of the Growth of Heaven*, and his brother, the woodsman Peter Boone, whose poems were never published. I also "translated" seven Romanian poets, all of whom, with one exception, I invented. I wrote their work in English, then translated it into the "original" Romanian. This manuscript was also never published, but I have a feeling that it isn't half bad; I'd like to re-read it one day. I also "invented" a very real person who had influenced me a great deal, even inspiring my idea of "inventing" him: Tristan Tzara. The famous Dadaist who was (and is) my inspiration, met in spirit with such near-contemporaries of mine as Frank O'Hara and Kenneth Koch, and my informal teacher, Ted Berrigan, to make literary activity fun, spontaneous and impish (as well as grave, socially relevant and criminally liable).

My collection of notebooks grew almost at the rate of my book collection. All that separated them was print, that elusive line between private and public. I already suspected that my notebooks' chief use would be storage in an Archives. In addition to thinking (less and less) that they might be of use to me, I started unconsciously listening for the sound of the future, for an archival bird-call. This was a transparent form of vanity; present, I realized, since my very first literary attempts.

[48] Writing is life for the time when one writes; but even then, it may only be partial if one is multitasking. Writing does not consume life, which is present and ongoing, it consumes only the remembered traces of it, the selective memories or feelings of the memories. In this sense, the writing life is the life that cleans up after itself, it dredges the refuse that refuses to go away, and it orders it in neat lines for disposal.

[49] For a technical attempt at describing just how words become flesh, see *whatever gets you through the night: a story of sheherezade and the arabian entertainments*:

> *Flesh was story in all its dimensions. Yes, Sheherezade discovered that words could be made flesh; storied characters became alive through telling and then stayed alive as long as they were told by others, dying only when they stopped traveling, when their seed dried up and their bodies shrank to nothing. The human body, her own body for that matter, was both a story-body and a flesh-body, and there was no telling where one ended and the other began; they were identical at all points. What she was seeking to discover was the fold-drive where the transfer of word to flesh took place, the infinitesimal point (the smallest she could think of) where a small tentacle exited the word to latch on to the next word with a protein.*

Knowing this, even as I forced myself not to articulate it, threw a bit of shadow into my writing, a filmy screen that, when added to the default screens already in place (like the one between life and writing[48]) made for a special opacity. I fought it but it was there, my public stance required it; the act of writing was a public act, why else do it, instead of just thinking it? Yet I was stubbornly attached to the idea of art as rebellion, the poet as a delirium machinegun firing words at injustice. The truth is ambiguous: I was not writing for any public, but in order to elucidate my own (constant) bafflement. Writing ordered my thoughts, it made sense of things I thought about and it also caused thoughts born out of itself that needed further writing to get fully thought. On the other hand, I believed (or wanted others to believe) that the enterprise itself was a dangerous guerilla operation at the root of expression that created, in various and mysterious ways, reality itself.[49] This function of poetry needed propaganda, so I put in extra time to polish my revolutionary credentials, even if others may have seen my exclamatory mode as a form of vanity. Well, I only hope that a true reader can clear this misunderstanding. Ha. A reader *intent* on clearing such a subtle misunderstanding would have to be a reader-for-pay, because why else would anyone work to so finely shave a writing mammal of its hairy vainglory? This future reader-for-pay (the only kind of reader in the future, I'm afraid) would be a sort of craftsman who removed not only the follicles of an archived writer's vanity, but also the veneer and mannerisms of his ancient influences who'd contaminated the genius with their ideas of order. My reader would be paid overtime to clear up all these blemishes, as well as other flaws of form better visible to herm in the future.

Such barbers the future has! Priceless, like MasterCard.
After all, I had always been misunderstood, since my
childhood in Sibiu, Oedipus before he became an adjective, seething brightly and sullen among antiquities,
all the way to that moment in my youth when I stood
speechless before beauty at Cafe Figaro. What I didn't
think at those times, but I nevertheless knew, was that
the line separating handwriting from print, the private
and the public, was going to be erased by the future,
and that only the misunderstandings would remain,
inkblots or typos of a clumsy past. I had no idea, after
I intuited this, how rapidly the computer would make
creating and publishing one and the same thing. Writing and publishing, talking and broadcasting were soon
going to be identical, leaving only the misunderstandings that writers had once hoped would be corrected
when words migrated from notebook to print, with the
help of editors, spell-checkers and legions of the professionals that tended in those days the transition between
the sloppy space of the notebook to the rigorous box
of the book. I didn't suspect that in less than a decade
such hopes would be quaint, intention would count for
nothing, and that only content (by weight) would have
any value at all. In that soon-to-come-future my paid
reader would question all the flaws and misunderstandings cleared in the past by armies of middlemen, and
herm might question as well the utility of such a job.
Read for what? To legitimize the value of a writer from
the end of an era that emphasized some sort of (in-
comprehensible) values embedded in a messy text? No
money would have made me do that then, leave alone
in the future, when there would be infinitely more en-
tertaining ways to kill time. It's not a mystery that artists are clairvoyant and often careless, but in one re-

spect we are exact and pitiless: our art is going to be the currency of the future.[50]

My Sixties contemporaries foresaw and practiced the erasure of the distinction between private and public, between "high" and "pop." Marshall McLuhan theorized it, and Andy Warhol practiced it. My notebook-personae project was not articulate in its beliefs, but it too had an intuitive trust in the zeitgeist; the times were working with me as long as I kept my old-world pretensions to a minimum. Still, posterity scared me, only because I thought of it now and then as the only payoff. I was against it, but some stubborn provincial part of me suspected that I was producing for a restricted-access public in the future, for a school kid just like me, open-eyed in wonder at the Astra Library. I was an 18th-century scrivener tormented by rain, lust and tuberculosis, hoping to be vindicated by the future. I'd brought the virus of metaphysics with me from insane old Europe and I worked hard to dispose of it. But what if I was wrong and the only evidence of my genius was this huge effort at killing the meta-yearnings of my poetry? How many poets stood upright in their graves with their hair in vertical fright when they saw future young scholars foraging through their papers on a library table? Thousands. All of them. They *lived*[51] for it. And when that fine mist

---

[50] In my workshops I limited the money supply thus: I paid $5 for every poem a student did not write, $3 for an unwritten story and $1 for an unthought essay. It cost me a bit, but what peace I gained! In addition, I made the writing itself valuable because if it was written despite my incentives against it, it was backed by the writer's strong belief in it, despite the financial loss. In this way, only the desperate originality of bohemians who couldn't help themselves was worth anything. Later, when the currencies of states lost credibility (the huge "Crisis of Confidence" of the years 2013-2027), you couldn't even get a cup of coffee without a poem. One of my descendants bought a whole side of beef for a three-volume novel in verse. See later footnote for detailed economics of poetry.

[51] Or *died*.

overcame the weary future researcher who must take off herm glasses and wipe them, unsure what's made everything hazy and why herm feels drowsy, it is the fine ash of incinerated scribblers protesting the only way they know how. The clearing of their opaqueness by a smart posterity had been, for better or worse, *a* (if not their whole) raison d'être. Until we made fun of all that.

When I moved to San Francisco in 1970, my little bit of notoriety and chutzpah put me in another poetic scene that produced maniacally all kinds of material, most of it scripted, but also many chapbooks, broadsides and full-sized books. At some point, every poet I knew had a mimeograph machine and a press that published their friends' works. We never thought our publishing ephemeral, and, as it turned out, it wasn't. Many of our amateurish (printing-wise) productions are more sought after now than perfectly bound collections then issued by "major" publishers. The atmosphere that favored our production was, again, a call from the future. All of this instant and continual literature ended up signed and lined up nicely on bookshelves I learned to build myself, or under tables, beds, on window-sills, and under later productions from the same sources. My own authored books, magazines, chapbooks and broadsides tried to separate themselves from the inky flood of my generation, but it was hard to do. Sometimes I set my own stuff in proper alphabetical order along my contemporaries, just like in a bookstore, and sometimes I put them on a special shelf that Ed Sanders once called laughingly, "the vanity case." And then he laughed and added, "What a great idea!" As if he, a prolific and wonderful author, had never thought of it!

The line between my "vanity case" and my notebooks was growing fainter and fainter. If there was still a difference, it is because the internet was still just an idea, and there were still editors. These editors (disciplinarians, jailers) were a visibly declining strain. We eliminated them when we became our own editors, and then editors of others who needed editors until they became editors and so on; the profession continued, but it was absorbed faster and faster by the producers, until the creative act and the critique acted (and were) as one. And then came the huge affirmation of the internet, and editors became a mere afterthought after pushing "Send." The Pop Age I had migrated to was America itself, a society that had privileged the esthetic of the machine; it was thus inevitable that the machine would dispense with human inefficiency in every field except the creative, where inefficiency is the seed-pod for future and better machines. Editors had been impediments, and (our) American culture eliminated them.

In 1973 at the Folsom Prison Library in California, I had a true editing moment. Folsom Prison, known among the cognoscenti as "the Harvard of prisons," had its library managed at the time by an Arnold Toynbee scholar, a pipe-smoking impeccably dressed man, who had been forced by the State of California to allow poets to conduct workshops in that famous institution. Built by Chinese prisoners just after finishing the railroad, Folsom Prison is a small city that looks Victorian and overwrought, as if the prisoners, having finished the prosaic modernist railroad, had given their lyric impulses full reign to polish and perfect each stone until streets and buildings shone like imperial jade. At least that was my first impression when I got a ride up to the stunning structure in the Sierra Nevada foothills, and contemplated the first inner courtyard from the window of the first of what turned out to be many control rooms. The librarian puffed patiently on a wooden bench while I was interrogated by a warden about my mission and identity. My mission was clear: I was there to teach poetry to criminals at the behest of the California Council for the Arts. My identity wasn't such an easy task: I didn't drive so I didn't have a driver's license. My ride had already left, and the only thing capable of vouching for me was a copy of *License to Carry a Gun*. Despite its unfortunate title, which made it look like I was smuggling a gun manual into prison, the cover displayed my picture: a long-haired hippie with a foot inside a garbage can on First Avenue in New York City. Throughout the discussion that followed on the question of whether such a picture on the cover of a poetry book can be considered a valid form of identification or not, I kept making desperate attempts to eye-contact the librarian who calmly smoked his pipe on the bench, steadfastly refusing my more and more desperate glances. Since the librarian didn't acknowledge me, and I refused to give up my indignant defense of poetry and photography, the exasperated warden picked up the phone and called his boss. His boss called a bigger boss, and, after what seemed like five hours, a very important Warden showed up, a man so giant he could have crushed both the librarian and myself with one hand. It was with that hand that he cracked open my sorely abused poetry collection and read quietly to himself several verses. Without looking at me, he then picked up the phone and said into it, "It's just fucking poetry, boss. Just fucking poetry!" With these words, the gates clanged open and I was steered along endless metal corridors to ornate courtyards that led to a small library in a building euphemistically called "the Adjustment Center." This "Adjustment Center" was the maximum security heart of the maximum security federal pen of Folsom. The AC was the permanent home of stars, Charles Manson and Sirhan Sirhan among them. On the way, I made conversation with the librarian, who turned reasonably affable after I had been positively identified. He was reticent as to the reading habits of Manson and Sirhan, a subject I was interested in, and answered instead by reciting long passages from Toynbee, which answered all questions, historically and forever. My Toynbee-quoting guide was also the prison censor, and he was more explicit on the matter of reading material he allowed to go through to prisoners: pornography (and experimental writing verging on it), no; most poetry, no; some philosophers (Hume) yes, some (Marx) no; some historians (Toynbee) yes, some (G. Legman) no; some psychologists (Skinner) yes, some (Wilhelm Reich) no. This sounded reasonably thoughtful, though it tended to exclude most of my favorite writers. I didn't argue. I won't recall here all that passed during my several "poetry workshops." (I already wrote all that in my 1976 memoir, *In America's Shoes*); I note this incident simply to explain the mixture of awe and dread that attended the verification of my identity by a jailer who may have been the last serious reader of poetry in the world to truly believe in the authority of the printed word; he had, after all, read a few verses before he picked up the phone. I know that "reader," as a species of animal that validates a published author, exists even now in the 21st century, but the specimen is contaminated by the knowledge that "print" is something anyone can commit. On the way to the prison library, the Folsom librarian did tell me that he had to deflect many "sick" collectors of killers' writings and art. This disclosure made the small library where he had a metal desk and a wooden stool, awesome to me. Lined up on perforated metal shelves were worn books that had provided the mental life of perps with centuries of imaginative material. Some of them had produced their own, and free people *collected* it. At the time, this gave me a chill that was part recognition: I had invented Julio Hernandez, a prisoner who wrote poetry. He hoped to be freed because the authorities recognized his talent— as did indeed happen to several prisoners in the political days of the Sixties—but he did not imagine being *collected*. In the end, Julio was freed by a circuitous route: Robert Bly, who believed that Julio was an innocent political prisoner and a great poet, proposed to publish him and work for his release. I felt obliged to tell Bly that I had made Julio up. Needless to say, Julio was never published by Robert Bly, and this great poet was set free (by me). I never wrote another Julio Hernandez poem. This might not have been the case, had I known that he was collectible; I might have made him an artist, too. The collecting craze was but a tiny spring in 1973, but it's grown considerably since. Charles Manson's art is sold openly by collectors, as are the prison works of any serial killers: the more gruesome, the higher the price. Punk and metal rockers collected them to enhance their image.[52] The collectors are not affiliated, as far as I know, with any library or museum, but should

[52] Killer art is at a premium, a kind of Viagra for the high finance death-wish. This latest wave is not in any way different from any other collectors. Collectors are not archivists, and collections are not archives: the object-hunting collectors are fetishists, and the objects themselves are totems, symbols that deliver private energy to their owners. There is no reason to disbelieve that these objects don't "deliver," even if they do not enlist themselves neatly in certified chronologies. They "deliver" because they are thwarted: instead of being components of a culture, they are isolated through violence (monetary, military, or fraudulent) and in the "thwarting" they release whatever power accrued to them when they were functional. The collector is an honest lone vampire; the archivist is a licensed vampire. A secret, fetishistic collection has very little public use, whereas an Archives is a school. Another paradoxical distinction between private collector and archivist is that the first declares herm sensual intentions from the start, while the archivist operates a hidden erotics under an ascetic cover. The "knowledge is ascetic" fallacy originated with eunuchs, monks, and self-mutilators, who evolved a non-reproductive, defensive approach to novelty that congealed into dogma. The success of pretend-nonsensual approaches to knowledge results in their teachability, a process in which the erotic encounter between monk and novice takes place hypnagogically between drowsiness and sleep, like sex between J. Edgar Hoover (collector of malignant information) shaving in the mirror while his assistant-lover Clyde showered erect behind the plastic curtain. The erotics of private collecting is recognized and vaguely shameful, while the eros of Archives is in the closet. In other words, collectors know that they are perverts, while archivists use the authorities to cloak their kinks.

an institution become interested they would do worse than to consult the former Folsom librarian who, if still alive, may, in retirement, relax his disclosure policies. Folsom's was both a public library (for prisoners with privileges) and an Archives of art and writing being made by criminals for a growing market of kinky collectors.[53] The art and writing of mental institution inmates has been currency since the Romantics, so it was no different in "regular" prisons: the line between "insanity" and "reason" was disappearing at the same rate and at the same time as the line between "manuscript" and "book."

In Baltimore in 1983 I founded *Exquisite Corpse: A Journal of Books & Ideas*, because I was bored and I felt anonymous despite my publishing "successes." The *Corpse* was a money-losing proposition, like most little magazines. In our paper existence (1983-1996), a long one in the history of unaffiliated little magazines, we published many 20th-century superstars, including William Burroughs, Allen Ginsberg, Diane DiPrima, Anne Waldman, James Broughton, James Laughlin, Edouard Roditi and hundreds of only less stellar poets, essayists and novelists, all of them at their polemical, combative, most youthful best, because that was the tone of the magazine. The modern and postmodern imperatives to, respectively, "make it new" and "get it used," became in our vision a call to "get it used to make it new." We changed the motto on the mast often, to suit each issue's whims. The first one was "Aim high, hit low," and, among my favorites, "Reproduction is forbidden but memorization is encouraged." City Lights Books in San Francisco published the first anthology from the magazine, *The*

[53] Coprophiliacs, actually; an ironic perversion death-row residents are proud of: the profit from their crimes will never equal the profit from the "shit" they make. If they were murderers, they had literally turned people into shit, and now their own literal shit turned to gold for other people. This is the miniature-scale model of the greater economy.

*Stiffest of the Corpse: 1983-1988,* followed by a two-volume anthology published by Black Sparrow Press in 1999/2000 in three editions: an A-Z hardcover numbered and signed by the editors (Laura Rosenthal & myself), a commercial hardcover edition, and a trade paperback. We were accumulating a treasure-trove of manuscripts, handwritten and typed, original art, letterpress broadsides, limited, numbered editions and correspondence.

The more I immersed myself in the poetic culture of a place, whether New York or Baltimore, my scriptural activity grew exponentially. I produced an immense quantity of written material, both of my own devising and in collaboration with others, and when I think that another medium of my literary life was for many years Talk, I thank the fates that Talk went on (mostly) unrecorded and untranscribed. Bars, cafes and restaurants were one archival repository of my thinking ("made in the mouth" as Tristan Tzara said) that never made it to paper. Still, my involvement in the scripted slivers of the infinite schism that is American poetry produced enough written material to fill a warehouse. Writing was my métier, Archives was (still) a future somebody else's problem, and while I still kept (and keep) journals (mostly jotting down ideas to be developed later) I published books of poetry, novels, essays; I edited anthologies; I wrote several newspaper columns; I wrote essays for radio, I wrote film scripts and considerations of art and architecture; I wrote speeches that were essays and essays that became speeches. I invented a form of prose-poem delivered as radio-essays on National Public Radio. When I started broadcasting, the audience for NPR's show *All Things Considered,* where I had my audio-column, was three million listeners. By 2011 it became thirteen million. My broadcasts began at the peak of the Gutenberg Age, and my fan letters (which I kept) came from ordinary people and specialists who pointed out the unthought-of directions of my thoughts, or their factual or conceptual mistakes; these letters numbered in the thousands. They were addressed to me.[54]

And then came the future: on internet blogs and discussion groups my writing acquired a life of its own: it was discussed, dissed and dissected without dealing with my physical person. My product acquired the kind of life that the Gutenberg Age used to grant only posthumously. In the Gutenberg Age a living writer was difficult to find and to interview, but in the Internet Age the interview over email became its own literary form, used not to elucidate previous work, but as additional "content" to fill out the increasingly capacious memory of the web. There was suddenly an imperious demand for further product. I loved it: every interview was an occasion for reinvention; it was like going to America over and over again. I gave hundreds of interviews where some of my (or my someone's) best thinking was. I can't guarantee the freshness of every creature, but hidden among my e-spawn were truly novel monsters quaking with stem-cell glee. In the transition between the McLuhan and Gutenberg ages, I invented another form: the blurb-poem. This came about as the result of a great demand by writers, known and unknown, to have their manuscripts read by a better-known writer who'd write something flattering about the book, to be printed on the back or front cover, the flap jacket, or on the page before the Acknowledgments. I was

[54] This may be the last "me" I can speak of without quotation marks, so keep this in mind, reader, when you encounter me henceforth out of quotes. The reason is that my accented English gave birth to numerous mishearings that my listeners found appropriate and deliberate; in some cases what they heard didn't even approximate what I said. The unbracketed me is naked because I am using it somewhat disingenuously to draw a border between the before and after of the internet: when people were not writing to me or to "me," they were writing to a voice on the radio; they were trying to be heard in the agora before the internet gave them a real, or a "real" voice. The border I drew in the main text is a feint, and only a trace in this footnote.

conscientious at first, reading every word of each manuscript or galley snail-mailed to me; I weighed my remarks to make sure that the reader understood what
was in the book and where the book stood in the vast
but knowable body of Literature. I was not unaware,
even then, that I was making a poem each time I wrote
a blurb, and I listened carefully for the music of my
aphoristic criticism. In the Internet Age blurbing also
took on a life of its own when I realized that it wasn't
necessary to read the PDF, or even the manuscript or
galley (not all of it, anyway); it was more important to
create a trenchant musical poem of such beauty that
it could stand alone. Often, instead of reading, I interrogated the book: I opened it at random and if the
oracular answer was satisfactory, it became the starting
point for my blurb-poem. I will not say that my blurb-
poems were often better than the books they pretended
to reference, but I seriously advise my future students
to look alertly at these. (I now feel haze around me
and have to wipe my glasses... OK, I'm back.) Other
writings, such as introductions to art and architecture
books, and travelogues for airline magazines (free trips
to exotic places) were contracted for profit, but I'm not
ashamed of them. I tried to not dumb down the writing
for the sake of the medium, but sometimes I expressed
myself in simpler and shorter sentences than I'd have
liked to. Throughout all these years of intense literary
and quasi-literary activity (1970—ongoing) I wrote
poetry, which I thought of, and still do, as the high-
est form of writing. My cerebral girlfriend from long
ago, who lovingly copied my first poems in her slanted
script, told me in an (intellectually) intimate moment,
"If you ever write a novel I'll never talk to you again!"
That was just before I left Romania at nineteen, and I

never saw her again, and never again did she speak to me.[55] But if ever I see her again she shouldn't be disappointed. I tried to keep as much poetry in my prose as is humanely possible and still get paid. My novels were a joy to write, full of things poems just hadn't room to hold. And the books themselves smelled good. That was before the BGS (Big Google Scan) or Kindle, before all books went down the rabbit hole of techne's will, to serve as kindling.[56]

I was hired by LSU in Baton Rouge in 1984, after two years of living and teaching in Baltimore. The boxed Codrescu books, manuscripts and letters followed dutifully along, reduced as severely as possible. Moving nearly two decades of frenetic literary activity was akin to moving a city. Measures had to be taken. The process of reduction would make a book-length essay in itself: a nightmare that wavered between a bonfire and a scholastic perpetuum-mobile. Short of an auto-da-fé, the number of angels knocked off the pinhead was a matter that would require a long Middle Ages to ponder, a scholastic era with monks working in silence. Without even noticing it I had become a Piler rather than a Preserver. I cleaved to some idea of order even as I lugged my considerable weight. Writings by myself were boxed separately from the writings of others to or about me (letters, articles, theses), but I stored these boxes together and called them unselfconsciously "my archive." There was stuff I didn't need, but I couldn't throw out—letters, for instance, from writers who'd chosen second-class celebrity by writing to me regularly in the hope of ending up in my Archives. Some of these letters were written by wonderful, playful people who wrote as well

[55] Not exactly true; I did speak once to Aurelia on the telephone. She had emigrated to Canada after marrying the only other Jew left in Sibiu, Max Fischer, the son of the tailor who made my high school graduation suit. She had two children by then, and never said, "If you're ever in Alberta..."

[56] Paradoxically, even as they were doing so, their numbers increased. There were more books published when it was suspected that there would be fewer readers than ever before. It was the fireworks finale of the Gutenberg Age. The computer made it easier to make "books," so writers didn't shy away from using the cause of their demise to hasten their end. The year 2000 marked in proper millennial fashion the grand efflorescence of the book's end, a death-wish made festive by their writers.

or better than famous authors. Reading these letters a future scholar might even think that they witnessed intimacy, an exchange between friends; herm might even abandon the addressee and follow the letter-writer without suspecting that it is a one-way road. These letters (if not their authors) are something of a mystery; I'm sure that they exist in every writer's archive, at least in every writer an intelligent but unlucky or unambitious guilder has decided is first rate and hence his glory gate; this kind of epistolero is a parasitic-symbiotic life-form that grows in the shadow of every (perceived) big tree. These letters may even fool the recipient, who thinks he has found a sensitive and smart reader, not realizing that he is not their intended target: the future is. The epistoleros use the light-refracting qualities of the famous to create their own oeuvre, to develop under the canopy; they are only using the addressee as a medium; their letters say "Dear Andrei," but they mean, "Hello, future! Look at my writing in these letters! See how better it is than your ostensible subject of study!" Even if I suspected such letters of using me as a foil, I couldn't get rid of them; they affirmed that I was the bigger tree, that others lived in my shadow; they made me *believe* that I was first-rate (they conceded it), and so I couldn't just chuck'em merely because they might slowly drain my future of the attention I deserve. The epistoleros are pretend-children, eerie and prescient beings that look innocent the better to suck you dry. Future scholars, when you are reading this essay, please do not be deceived by these flatterers like I (nearly) was! Nobody is flattering *you*, future scholars, so keep your eyes on the ball! Of course, a good investigator will quickly smell a rat: these are mostly one-way letters, rarely answered. Even in the pre-internet days one can see that these letters haven't been answered: they are beautifully written accounts of the epistolero's life, referencing the recipient only when a major event occurs, a book, a prize... then there are congratulations, astute insights about the great progress of this new book or the importance of that prize... and then it's back to the epistolero's Promethean blog of self projecting itself into the future, refracted through your lens.

Little did I know in 1984 that my vision of a quiet meditative life as a minimalist poet-professor will turn out instead to be the open floodgate for an entire new writing career, dragging in its wake hundreds of new papers, publications, correspondence, photographs, audio and videotape, art, diplomas, plaques, and fetishes. Part of my vision of the meditating prof lost in thought strolling through campus fleurs (and this, being Louisiana, there isn't a time when the fleurs aren't fleuring) was spending time in the library reading poets I didn't know. I imagined that after years of active participation on the poetry scene, I would sit down with the poets of the past (or from alien gangs) and fill what I felt to be lacunae in my education. Then I would become penitently silent, to slip, relaxed and melancholy like a falling leaf into the history of literature.

Two of my students stand (archivally) out. The first, a shy schizophrenic, found poets insufferable in their claims to uniqueness. He made it his job to circle in pencil the numeral "1" or the word "one" in every poetry book and literary journal in the LSU library. When he was done with the few thousand volumes at our university, he took on other libraries, including those of some of the biggest universities with the largest collections.

In the end, he must have hit all poetry in English and English translation, all modern and contemporary poets[57], and thousands of magazines that published poetry. It's a fair bet that many of these books with circled "1"s and "one"s are still on library shelves, because it would have been impossible to replace the books or erase all the pencil marks, even if all had been found.[58] "One" must have thought his work complete after two years of intense poetry hunting: he committed suicide. His parents established a poetry award in his name.

The other student, a brilliant bilingual writer, an American raised in France, also had a quarrel with books, though he wrote two superb volumes of enigmatic short stories. Everyone anticipated his next writings, but we heard nothing more from him. A few years later he reemerged as a celebrated computer hacker who used his artistic imagination[59] to perform social justice cyberstunts. He used new media to mirror, confound, and derail corporations and institutions on the internet. He produced sites that invited either redirection, without

[57] Poets who escaped the touch of "One," as I called him, have been privileged by obscurity or being "checked out," and belong to a special tribe that, should they become known to each other, ought to hold annual celebrations.

[58] The hunt for the marked books might still be going on, providing thousands of jobs.

[59] Imagination reprised: I have often said that I have no imagination. This assertion is meant to be understood as an insistence on reportage, facts, and commentary on what they could possibly mean (a critical faculty). Imagination is masturbatory, the projection of self into virtual worlds shaped like bodies. Even the occasional projection of this sexualized shape into other forms, sheep, let's say, is imprecise and funny. (Not to the masturbator, of course.) Religion, including the religion of poetry, has capitalized Imagination to mean that a dreamer can be a demiurge ("un pequeño dios"), but the physical limits of how many projections a "self" can produce end with the body. The imagination of machines is infinite, even if they resemble the original projectionist. The human self derives pleasure from its doubling, tripling or multiplying flesh, the projection of its mirroring, but it is limited to single digits. The machined self produces replicas that can elicit pleasure and illumination, but the self becomes a helpless spectator to these virtualities, seeing "something like itself," a repetitive hell. The spectating self eventually dies from the pain of spectating its reproduction, but its machined theatre continues ad infinitum, skeuomorphically maintaining the original form of the "self" that once imagined and never returned from that imagining.

ever returning to a central place, or self-destruction, like Tinguely sculptures.[60]

Both these students, "One" and "Web Bandit," were looking at books as being constituted to falsify reality. And they took measures. Beyond the clinical and political aspects, their suspicion of books corresponded with my ambivalence about teaching poetry. When I saw poetry as an instrument of revolution via language, I felt the need to dynamite the prevailing academic canon with my own. My own was a personalized version of thousands of not-yet-prevailing canons loaded and waiting for their turn to canonize. I published anthologies. Breaching the walls of academia with new canons was child's play in the Nineties: the walls were already perforated by the innumerable free-lance canoneers who'd been besieging the English Department for the last four decades of the 20th century. Still, the English Department held—even as Jews, minorities, avantgardists and demolitionists poured in from all areas of the Humanities. Some of the assault vanguard had been waiting so long its soldiers died before their canons were ever fired; they were splendid baseball pitchers aging in the minor leagues while waiting for old men on steroids to retire from the majors. While waiting, they mixed metaphors. And drinks. Lots of drinks. Some of the assaults were dadaistic: erasure, for example, of consecrated text to make new text out of it, *vide* Ronald Johnson's erasure of *Paradise Lost* to create *Radios*, or Tom Phillips' *Humument*, an erasure of the Victorian novel *A Human Monument*. Others used books as oracles, elements of sculpture, performance aids or furniture. Some writing turned into paintings, paintings turned into sculpture, sculpture turned into music

[60] One of his works was a mirror site for a major internet company: inquiries addressed to the company came to the mirror-site, and the orders for goods were translated into poetic objects that were returned virtually; another site mirrored a major international affairs association, and requests for speakers were honored by their creator, who dressed in a suit and flew to various meetings of this respectable assembly, and presented scientific-sounding arguments of sheer poetic absurdity. He was often applauded, and never caught, until bored with the ease of fooling so-called "financial experts," he blew his cover in a documentary film. From there, the media virtuoso branched into areas that cannot yet be discussed.

(pace Valéry), music turned into stone, stones took the microphone. These assaults sound nostalgic now, like the siege of Troy; when the English Department finally crumbled, it beseeched the besiegers to save it: all genres and genders rushed in to be hastily institutionalized. The obvious and honorable thing would have been to surrender and abolish the job of teaching writing and literature, but then where would I get another one. If asked, I said that my job was to be a guide for pointing students to the poets I loved. The textual world seemed inevitable to me, either way. At times, I confined myself to explaining why I loved some poets, a process that helped me love them again, and better. This was a comfortable role, the line of least resistance, but I found it often unsatisfactory. In my heart of hearts I believed that poetry, far from "changing nothing," changed everything, but how it did that was the mystery that was in effect poetry's only subject. The intimacy with language that an individual might acquire in practicing this art was not cozy, and it was not for the benefit of improving either language or the individual, but rather a symbiosis between them, which involved changing the world (as we know it, and *en passant*). In this light, the actions of "One" were gentle remonstrances to poets who used the first-person singular, a reminder that their "self" is not why they were in business. The fact that he used a pencil, not a magic marker or other indelible instrument, and he did not hunt down poets to tattoo them, for instance, shows that he was a gentle soul. He could have been a physical scourge out of Dante's Hell or the Inquisition, but he committed no (great) violence against either books or their writers; he simply emphasized the numeral, a tender, ironic means of telling readers that the author had misunderstood herm mission, which was to change the world, and only incidentally to write poems. His suicide surely had its own logic, but one might see it as despair at the sheer enormity of the task of marking every poetry book in the world; there are millions, more than can be uncovered in a lifetime, all of them written by individuals, "ones" who never rose, in his view, above their singular vision. I am assuming a great deal here because I'm still in thrall to the military metaphors I grew up with: poets, in this view, were avant-garde, main body and rear-guard, all three fighting bodies arraigned before a series of peepholes through which they viewed the enemy; each peephole was the perch of an individual "I" who described the enemy in herm own idiosyncratic language. Perhaps my suicide felt that these poetic legions were looking at *him* and that he was "the enemy." If so, he had no choice but to poke out every cyclopean eyeball with the tip of his pencil. Or, obversely, he may have intuited that the three divisions (avant, main and rear), were not looking out at any outside enemy, but were watching each other. If this was the case, he would have been completely outside the viewing arena, an enemy without an enemy, watched by no one. His pencil marks would have been shy signals then, waves of his depressed hand: Hello there, "one" who's book I'm holding, I am the unwatched enemy! And when, having marked (almost) every poetry book in the world, there was still no acknowledgment from the troops, he had no choice but to kill the enemy: himself.

My other pupil left books behind altogether in order to act on ideas that would have been confined to paper forever if the internet hadn't been there. These ideas

were internet ideas; even if they'd had the reach of the
Communist, Dada, Surrealist or Situationist manifestos, they'd have had but half the efficacy the internet
age granted them. The internet activist, far from surrendering, could handle the paradoxes of self: he "fleshed
out" pieces of himself in collective actions and actions
that changed collective "I"s into cyber-"we"s. In the
20th century, as far as the 1980s, the activist could have
fallen prey to the rhetorical traps of stalinism and mao-
ism, but the insistence of poetry saved him from that.
After the physical collapse of rhetorically-based communist societies, one could only act poetically in the
interests of the collective, that is to say, absurdly, paradoxically and cognizant of the techne. Any affective intrusion into the logic of the machine had to be superbly
intelligent. The poetic activist had what it took, my sad
schizophrenic didn't.

Both of these young men were affected by the religion
of poetry. The chief ritual of this religion is storytell-
ing by possessed humans who are experiencing a state
of hyperlucidity (aka, writing). The words of the possessed are simultaneously transcribed by the hyperlucid
scribe. These states of being coexist in poets without
cancelling one another—au contraire, the lucid thinker
watches the drunk with awed delight, spurring herm
to greater heights (depths). The result, poetry, is a collaboration between the demon who possesses the poet
and the intelligence that studies it. Let's call the god
for whom this ritual is performed Pan, the nature-god,
for the sake of simplicity. Pan is often the most poetic
deity. I had been infected with this religion in my youth
by poet/philosophers Eliade, Blaga and Tzara; after
reading them, I took for granted the outsider status

of poet/shamans who moved in a psychic wilderness where others were lost.[61] This religion predated its institutionalization, and even writing, though hyperlucidity had always been present, even without signing itself. By the time I started teaching, wilderness, psychic and environmental had mostly disappeared. No matter what any poet imagined, there was simply no longer any room for a critical conversation with divine intoxication. The hyperlucid self pretty much killed the drunk and took over writing; the words on the poetry page were no longer (or only faintly) those of the delirious medium. The hyperlucid state of writing closed off the "doors of perception" one by one, like a conscientious butler in a restaurant that had once been Pan's orgy cave, and then pulled the plug on the intoxicated music of the possessed. It was this activity of the hyperlucid self that "One" identified and started hunting with his pencil. He must have concluded that the march of the smug "I," of the "1" and "one," over the babble of the divine was unstoppable. The only thing that was in his power to stop was himself. Each "1" and "one" he'd circled was, nonetheless, a victory, a sign that he had discovered another infidel. He pointed to enough occurrences of arrogant singularity to warn the future of the serious predicament of the religion of poetry, which suffered from the fatal illness of the writing self. And he left us, of course, his unfinished task. Anyone who still believes in the religion of poetry must pick up the pencil and continue his work. There are innumerable books out there waiting for his disciples. "One" lives, make no mistake about it. No, I don't want to know who you are, just do your job, OK?

To keep my academic visibility[62] I continued editing my

[61] The religion of poetry worships AS (Aristotle - Spinoza), symbolized by a worm-tracked walking stick, or ASS (Aristotle-Spinoza-Satan) symbolized by a penis-knobbed worm-tracked walking stick.

[62] In order to hide my eyeball peering through the peephole.

Dada-tinged magazine, which became quite influential despite my best efforts. At its Baltimore beginnings, *Exquisite Corpse* conducted in its eclectic and hooligan-ish ways various assaults on the rear-guard academia and the "mainstream," the entities that my friends and I felt must be annihilated before any piece of the tiny pie of contemporary letters could be ours. I continued editing the *Corpse* when I became an LSU professor (to make a living), and I made (clumsy) attempts (as noted) to learn to tolerate the enemy, or at least read and write about poets my actual poetic project found boring. But like my dreams of a reflective and quiet life, the magazine belied this utopian vision; it was anything but tolerant and quiet; it stayed, as always, controversial. I had hoped to effect some collaboration between the publication and the institution (i.e., they would pay for it) but it became clear that the conservative administration would never accept the troublemaker. I had no intention of reigning in the *Corpse*'s glorious mayhem, so I separated it from my academic address. A Vice-Chancellor complained that we'd published an obscene drawing: clearly, she didn't read (things worse than that drawing lived there). We were read, subscribed to, commented on and did quite well despite the perpetual lack of money. *The Southern Review*, a staid quarterly of another age, with which we incidentally shared a hallway, was endowed to the gills by our university. I proposed that we mingle names for one issue: they could be the *Southern Corpse* and we could be the *Exquisite Review*. It was only the fact that the editor I had proposed this to did not carry a knife that I type this now.[63]

[63] Actually, one of the editors at the time was a gentle, old-fashioned soul who wore tweed outside and inside, and was proud of the traditionalism of *The Southern Review*, which was still (in 1987!) published by letter-press (!). In retrospect I admire this, but not the founding esthetic of the review edited by Robert Penn Warren and Cleanth Brooks with T.S. Eliot's wind (bag) in their sails. In 1987 Southern "gentility," the Great White Way, and thinly veiled xeno-phobia still rippled its pages gently, where once they'd been roiling. (Flapping veils, roiling pages! Sail on, ship of Murk!) At the 50th anniversary bash for *The Southern Review*, an ancient Cleanth Brooks chose as the subject of his talk a defense of T.S. Eliot's essays, *After Strange Gods*, and said that Eliot's remark that there are too many "free-thinking Jews" referred to free-thinkers, not to Jews, to which a reasonable voice in the audience asked, "If he meant free-thinkers, why did he say Jews?" Anyway, no one would have accused the tweedy editor of 1987 of such sentiments, but I was reminded, in the context of a possible cutup exchange of titles between our journals and the potential knife, that this man *actually* cut off the tip of his finger while chopping an onion, and instead of saving it on ice and calling a doctor, he flushed it down the toilet, bandaged the finger, and continued chopping. If he'd heard of reattachment, a fairly common procedure, he did not recall it when it came right down to it, which means simply that he, like *The Southern Review*, was not of our time. Shortly after emigrating, in 1966, I enrolled in a course on Dante at Wayne State University in Detroit; it was taught in Italian by a closeted gay man who, upon hearing from me that I wrote poetry,

78

Ah, hopeless dreams of the autodidact! The golden age, like all utopias, including the one I'd had the good fortune of escaping from in Romania, was being usurped, even as I dreamed it, by my own energetic efforts to inject literature with wit, and the opposition was stronger than I'd imagined. In the end, however, we were both, avantgarde and academy, doomed. There was a new technology in the world, a force that resolutely ended the Gutenberg Age, and did so at an inconceivable speed. The Print Age was over and we were fighting one of its last battles on an abandoned field.

Like a junkie, I couldn't help sliding into what was once called "cyberspace" (echo of the Cold War), but I kept as many papers as I could: old notebooks, non-electronic letters from friends, especially writers; I threw everything paper-made (including printed e-texts) into the same bins I threw my electricity and gas bills, so every time I moved I had to purge the mundane stuff and try to keep only what looked of possible interest to my literary life. I organized these documents vaguely by date and stacked them in boxes I taped shut. I never revisited the boxes when I got to a new place; they stayed taped shut, serving as coffee tables, room dividers or shelves for the new books sure to arrive desperately for review or just attention. I slid into the posthuman like a fly holding on to the flypaper it believes keeps it from falling.[64]

By the time of David Fauld's discovery of the Renata Pescanti Boti book-notebook, I had become a Piler. I was no longer a Preserver. In his purest form, the Preserver had disappeared with the loss of my first notebook. No longer aware at every moment of the

invited me to his house in the suburbs to show me his own poetry. Dressed in a resplendent robe he led me to a formal waiting room where I sat stiffly for an hour among naked marble Greek wrestlers while the sounds of a muted but violent argument between two men wafted through the floral wallpaper. When my teacher finally emerged, he apologized for his "roommate's temper," and handed me a copy of *The Southern Review*, which had just published his astral-inspired lyric *Andromeda* (or maybe it was called *Orion*, I forget). In any case, I left the Detroit suburb clutching this stellar reverie, and this was, until I started teaching at LSU, the last time I or anyone I know, mentioned *The Southern Review*. To my contemporaries it was so hopelessly square it just didn't exist.

[64] A metaphor culled from the 1950s.

location of my writing, I merely piled new stuff on a shelf, or anywhere else. Notebooks, typed poems, scraps scribbled on paper bags, menus or napkins, correspondence, "diskettes," disks, drives, tape cassettes, reel-to-reel audio tape, CDs, DVDs, were all deposited more or less on top of one another on any available surface. My public appearances, reading, lecturing, talking, left behind photographs, film and audio tape joining papers and computer files to make a three-dimensional, moving mess that either time dragged me through or I dragged behind me moving forward. Every time I moved, my waves of document, notes, manuscripts, letters, tapes, drives, rolled along. I hath become Okeanos clad in a suit of nymph-algae. Oddly enough, a new storage technology also appeared every time I moved, for the seeming purpose of consolidating the growing mess, but created instead more objects of its own that had to be added to previous ones. Thus, a paper correspondence might be scanned unto a disk, the disk entered into a computer's hard drive, but then there were more things on the disk than the correspondence, and more things on the drive than on the disk, so each new storage device tagged along more matter, even as it contained and miniaturized all that came before it. "Memory sticks" appeared, looking like lighters, just when I was trying to quit smoking, and I often tried absent-mindedly to light a cigarette with a 2 GB stick containing all my writing. I was giddy at the thought that all the books I had left behind in Romania could have fit in my faux-lighter. The meanness of the communists who forced us to leave Romania with nothing but a suitcase, now seemed like a joke. But the "memory stick" was a feint. Technologies did not replace each other, they merely swallowed each

80

others' contents, leaving intact the previous product inside its obsolete container. I lost new devices all the time, and just to make sure, I carried my handwritten notebooks, typed manuscripts, black binders, disks, diskettes, hard drives, computers and "memory sticks." As I write this, all I have ever made out of words is in a cloud. My hands should be free. They should be like the open empty palms you hold out to show someone that you're unarmed. See? All my stuff is in the Cloud, I can retrieve it any time. But this isn't how it is: my hands are raw from holding the straps keeping the huge shell of my products on my bent back. Instead of lifting my burden, the stuff I made has turned me into an upside-down pyramid whose tip writes this. I could never forget my first and lost notebook: it is the only unique object made of potent first words, and it is *lost*. It is like God losing herm's first command, "Fiat Lux," which, had it been lost, God would have forever wondered what herm'd said. And one wonders, post facto, if "lux" had dawned at all if the word had been lost. When the technologies of storage became identical with the technologies of production, all my new work went from the keyboard to the hard drive, then to the printer to make a paper copy, then directly into the computer's "archive," the second best-known word in English now after the word "google." My Gmail archive is not, of course, the same as my Archives; in the e-Archive, there is room for my pre-computer product *and* my new e-written one—and they both got *smaller* until they were taken up in a cloud.[65] The only things that stayed big (and on earth) are the non-e-notebooks and the manuscripts of the pre-computer age, which now look as huge and empty as Renata's poetry book looked to me when I started filling in its blank spaces. Poetry

[65] Typical of the archiving and shrinking is the following request by a digital Archives, which promises both fidelity to the original formats and an eternal afterlife, CLOCKSS, "a trusted community-governed archive" (www.clockss.org):

*The CLOCKSS Archive would like to invite **Exquisite Corpse** to join its growing list of participating publishers that are archiving their content for future generations. CLOCKSS (Controlled Lots of Copies, Keep Stuff Safe) is a not-for-profit joint venture among the world's leading scholarly publishers and research libraries, whose mission is to build a sustainable, geographically distributed dark archive with which to ensure the long-term survival of Web-based scholarly publications for the benefit of the greater global research community. Content is protected and stored in a closed network at 12 major research libraries located around the world and is only accessible in the event that it is no longer available from you. Publishers and librarians have equal say in deciding procedures, priorities, and when to make content available. That makes this archive the most likely to persist in the future as technologies and priorities change. By depositing your content into the CLOCKSS Archive, you can ensure the preservation of*

itself, by leaving space after each line and between lines, seemed like an enormous hollow cave that could fit millions of microchips filled with all of humanity's writings. And that had been poetry's purpose all along: the typesetter who first invented verse by breaking the continuous line of print had created storage space for the future. What he had not foreseen was that the future would not take its place quietly in the hollows (or "hallows") of Renata's book (which could have been the only Archives in the world) but was making its own (smaller and smaller) devices and frames to contain whatever it had to say. The net result was that the poor nomad of the late 20th century dragged after himself the paper weight of his writing and history, while the open jaws of content-hungry devices needing to be filled chased him as they multiplied, increasing the weight by psychic tons. To get away from the content-hungry machines he had to produce and run from production, all the while dragging his archive on his back and in the cloud above his head. Sweet freedom, lightness of being, etc, where are you?

In 1996 I took the *Corpse* online (www.corpse.org). Internet publishing was still a fairly unusual thing in those days. There were only a few literary magazines in "cyberspace." Blogs hadn't yet appeared, and Google was a gleam in the eye of the future. Renamed online *Exquisite Corpse: A Journal of Letters & Life*, the journal recreated itself with a new design each issue by the brilliant Andrea Garland. From 1984 to 1996, while still a print magazine, my editorial helpmate in the huge job of editing the *Corpse* was Laura Cole Rosenthal, now Laura Codrescu. Laura brought to the *Corpse* a sophistication that came from being the daughter of a librarian. Her

*your publications and reports. You will join the international, community-governed archive of librarians and publishers working together. The CLOCKSS Archive utilizes award-winning technology developed by Stanford University. It is different from other archiving services and platforms because it is only a dark archive, and your digital content will be preserved in the form published by you, rather than a "screen scrape," which is dependent on the current technologies/formats in use at the time of archive. The CLOCKSS archiving method ensures that today's content will be readable by tomorrow's scholars. Another differentiation is that once the dark archive is triggered there is free access to everyone, not just those libraries that hold subscriptions.*

mother, Fran Cole, had defied the odds of Louisiana provincialism and caused a splendid library to be built in West Baton Rouge Parish. Laura is an avid reader who found the public library an oasis of peace, calm and stability. The frantic din of *Corpse*-making tested her appetite for solitude, but she went along with it, until we stopped publishing on paper and went online. She stopped being interested at that time and, like a pedestrian going home, she walked against the current of internet traffic that soon swept everyone and everything in its swell. Laura's retreat to her library may have looked peaceful to her, but it was complicated for me. In 1996, Laura was replaced (in publishing) by a webmistress, Andrea Garland. Andrea was a tattooed New Orleanian whose body was her resume, the archive of her life and of her artistic tastes. Her tattoos were, for the most part, abstract, marking the mid-Nineties transition between the representational tats of an earlier age that commemorated deaths, loves and mortal professional associations (the Navy, the Hell's Angels, the SS) to new artistic aspirations that were more abstract and philosophical. Andrea's skin-pictures were significant to her history, as tats had always been, but they were also statements of style and essays on her thinking. She was a mystic and an activist who saw her job as designer of *Exquisite Corpse* as an extension of her skin. We were her literary tat. Andrea was among the first to bond physically with the alphabet, with the incised script that was older (and newer) than handwriting. Later, I saw others displaying tats of Hebrew letters or Celtic knots, Chinese proverbs, cosmogonic-mystical symbols, cuneiforms, gothic signs of death and afterlife, but Andrea was first in that transition, just as the *Corpse* was among the first journals to go online from print. Andrea was also pierced in ways and places that combined classic Gothic with New Orleans carnivalesque.[66] She brought to the design of the *Corpse* her edgy, dark extension that foresaw the bookish doomsday of the coming millennium while wallowing energetically in our orgiastic fin-de-siècle. Andrea was also in the vanguard of internet technology that she understood and used like a native tongue, the same as the language of her tats.[67] Her pretty

[66] Tats were to the Nineties and the first decade of the 21st century what long hair and hippie drag were to the Sixties. The differences are worth noting: while hair can be cut and clothes changed, tats are mostly forever. Differences notwithstanding, the tattooed tribes continued the utopian and sexual hippie esthetic, adding to it gothic, pop images, and social statements. A few weeks after Hurricane Katrina I saw a beautiful girl walking in the French Quarter in New Orleans with "504," the New Orleans area code, tattooed on her right arm. It has been my fantasy to have my poems incised on a body (or several) and to give a poetry performance by reading my nudes. Obviously a selfish feudal fantasy, because the incised words would mean more to me than to the incised. More to the point is a collaborative poem written by an audience in New York that came to hear me lecture on "the exquisite corpse" form at the Drawing Gallery, where an exhibition of artists' "exquisite corpse" collaborations was being shown. My "lecture" consisted of choosing (by means of pulling a name out of a hat) a young man from the audience and having the audience write on him with magic markers; then everyone read him simultaneously. Bodywriting is shaman art: the medicine man wrote spells on the skin of people possessed by demons. Never quite forgotten, skin writing was re-employed variously in the recent past; the poet Hannah Weiner literally read words on people when she looked at them. Her gaze was a little eerie, but, in the end, instructive. Photographer Miriam Waterman called on her subjects to choose which word(s) best represented them, then she applied these words herself to their chosen skin surface, and photographed it; she called her work "self-representation," but it was a performance initiated by her for her camera. In asking her subjects to think of a single word or phrase that represents their "self," she asked, in effect, for language-performances for her solo viewing pleasure. The words and bodies belonged only apparently to their subjects: the calligraphy and composition were hers. This form of orgiastography is said to have originated in the Storyville district of New Orleans in the 18th century, when men armed with quills and cocktails covered a whore with writing and awarded her to the best reader. This particular (and often permanent) means of note-taking has revived in a time when technologies of notation are multiplying through one's pocket phone, which is capable not just of taking notes, but of broadcasting them. The phone-cum-tattooing stylus is surely the next gadget: a spider-phone that walks all over one's body, inscribing it as instructed. Order one now: I'm building it as I write.

[67] The missing link between Andrea's tats and incised skin in general, is a novel use of digitization. A scanner device could "read" an inscription, especially an abstract one. An actual screen translation of symbols from a surface (pages in this case) was created by a Siglio Press book-object (2012), described by Christian Bök as follows:

*Between Page and Screen has reinvented visual poetry, doing so by displaying hieroglyphs that humans can read only through the eyes of robots. Each coded sigil resembles one of the cellular automata that a mathematician might find in the game of life—except that each glyph has become a cipher for an epistle that explores the sound of words, then explodes these messages into shrapnel. Such a book heralds the virtual reality of our own poetic future, when everyone can read a book while watching it play on television, each hologram standing in its cone of light, hovering above the open page.*

name, Garland, resonated with my own original name, Perlmutter (mother-of-pearl), Jewish pseudonyms from the same area of decorative cover. Her parents might have been horrified by the lush canvas of her body and told her that she'd never "work in the front office," but the "front office" had changed, along with the techne of printing. All the real work, including meetings, would soon be done in the secret enclaves of one's home or tribal den. The front office morphed into a space where a living human Archives representing both history and style welcomed its supplicants. The unlucky front office died, but the receptionist became a work of art. The customer/supplicant no longer needed to pretend to look through magazines: herm could wait dreamily reading a warm body that spoke as well as attracted.[68] Herm could wait in a room dominated by a living Archives on display, not hidden like the psychological archive covered by glossies and a social uniform. Andrea's "looks," her novel designs for the internet *Corpse* changed the journal, in essence making it young again; it set the literary polemic squarely in the present. Making the transition from print to e-publishing demanded a whole new outlook that was also brought about by my first Internet Age in-office assistant, Jean Lee, who performed the new and quickly evolving techne with

---

[68] Andrea, or aspects of her, served as the character Felicity in my novel *Messiah* (Simon & Schuster, 1999), where she is half the Messiah, the other half being a young woman actually called Andrea, for whom a young woman named Felicity modeled. Yes, I was something of a joker in those days. Felicity was not a real woman, but a character from a novella I wrote in 1976. This sort of self-referential injoking comes naturally to me—I see it as a sort of brick-laying, a layering of real and invented things that add up, when they do, to an architecture. On the other hand, given the "missing link" above, as seen *between page and screen*, Andrea could be "read" by a computer and reprinted as a text in any font or form the user might choose: as an ode, an elegy, a comedy, a novel, a screenplay, etc. The basis for the forms of "reading" her would be Raymond Queneau's *Exercises in Style* (translated by Barbara Wright; New Directions, 1981). In fact, she could be lived with and through, made love with, and taken to parties and to dinner at any stage of her skin-pictures through the use of a 3-D printer with Life Plus.

force and skill. The light-table disappeared, as did the mock-up. Gone too were mind-boggling "orphans and widows" (spaces left in pasting) that had made possible the discovery of Mike Topp, a poet whose short works fit miraculously. Gone were the lengthy conferences with printers who never understood our complex graphic requirements, poetry line breaks, the importance of unjustified spaces. Typesetting and design became a computer skill that made it possible for Jean and Andrea to replace an entire company of burly men at the print shop on whose good-will and union-rules we had depended. Producing the magazine on the computer made the existence of all the paper around us stifling and guilt-producing. We no longer needed it but it was important. We started drowning in our own history at the office, just as I was drowning in my own manuscript archive and books at home. The time had come to deposit this paper-and-plastic mountain into a "sanctioned" Archives.[69] Sanctioned by whom, you might do well to ask. The answer is: by anybody with the room, the money. Room and money don't add up

[69] For many years, I also practiced "archiving by lending," by which I mean that I lent my favorite books and sometimes copies of work-in-progress to students and friends I thought should read them. Needless to say, they never returned them. Still, they may have kept them, which means that a "dispersed archive" exists and can surface at any moment. This "dispersed archives" contains also numerous heated notes written for one desperate reason or another. The "dispersed archive" deserves its own essay/memoir, perhaps in a long footnote (since it's so blurry); this is why you find only the "sanctioned archive" in the main text. Footnotes are themselves a "dispersed archive." There is also an "Absent Archives," an unreachable body of document that was "dispersed" or "disappeared" before it was collected; this differs from the Archives of Amnesia because it is randomly, not deliberately, suppressed. A March 27, 2012 post concerning "archival silences" at www.archivesnext.com, by Anne-Marie Conde, offers a perfect example of both an Absent and a Dispersed Archives:

*The Australian War Memorial has a large collection of letters from enlisted personnel (especially from the First World War) sent to families and friends at home. These have been collected by the AWM since the mid-1920s. The replies – the letters to soldiers from wives, mothers etc – are not there. They may not have been kept by the soldiers (who often aren't able to carry large amounts of stuff with them); they may have been lost after the war; and on the whole they have not been sought by the AWM. In casual and not so casual ways the voices of the men 'at the front' have been privileged over those who wait at home. You can write the history of those who waited at home – it has been done – but it is a lot harder. This is a true, almost irreversible archival silence and it happened long before we ever started to think about digitization.*

The ArchivesNext site is concerned at this time with misunderstandings between digital researchers and archivists, and raises current issues about the different uses of the word "archive(s)" by humanists, historians, literary scholars and archivists. Recovering "dispersed" or "absent" archives is far in the future, and may require yet another professional specialization that will bring its own questions to the table.

to "sanctioned," but this is where vanity introduces a metaphysical dimension, an ego deformation attributable to the loss of my first notebook, which itself was a compensatory attempt to kill my stepfather[70]. The word "sanctioned" contains both the sense of "punished" and "sanctified." Losing it meant that my first attempt had failed (a punishment), and that all subsequent compensatory production had to be "sanctified" to make up for the loss and fulfill the original intent. This is why the "dispersed archive" in the footnotes has no place in this (main) text: it lacks the official patriarchal (the archon's) imprimatur.[71] The punishment could have taken many forms, loss being only one of them, but the sanctifying could come only from an institution.[72]

My first encounter with an archival library occurred at the University of Oklahoma, in Norman, where the jury for the Neustadt Prize, which included Susan Sontag and myself, was given a tour of what its custodian touted as the greatest History of Science Library in the US. This librarian's slight figure did not begin to intimate the defensive dimensions to which his body could swell to while displaying his treasures. He warned us that: a) the copy of Sir Isaac Newton's *Philosophiæ Naturalis Principia Mathematica*, published 5 July 1687 and hand-annotated by Newton himself, which he opened at random, was not to be touched by anyone present in whatever manner whatsoever, not even wearing the white gloves he himself was wearing, and b) that given the long study he had made of this collection, it was clear that "science" as we know it began its history in Greece, from a thought by Heraclitus. The copy of *Principia* reminded me suddenly of the

[70] A distinction here between "father" and "stepfather" is in order: killing one's father is the pure oedipal crime, while killing one's "stepfather" is more of a garden-variety crime, but also more appropriate in these times.

[71] Unless the "Dispersed Archive" is the new condition of patriarchy: a dispersal of authority throughout culture, a collective, fragmented authority that can never, like Humpty Dumpty, be made to convincingly stand for the whole abstracted glyph.

[72] The Library, the Church, the Tribunal.

chained incunabulum in the Astra Library of my youth, with the traces of *Tristan and Isolde*. Independent of my will, my eye found an opening between the librarian's gently pointing gesture and the elbow of his too-tight jacket, while my hand, also independent of my will, shot through the gap to touch with two fingertips Sir Isaac Newton's handwriting. You can imagine the indignation that followed. All I could mumble in my defense was: "I'm a poet." It seemed evident to me, somehow, that it is a poet's duty to sensually experience the handwriting of a genius. Happily, this breach of the curator's first warning was almost instantly followed by another, when Susan Sontag objected as only she could, to the idea, absurd to her, that science began in Greece with Heraclitus. There arose a debate that anyone familiar with Sontag's debating style could only be described as a rhetorical triumph of ignorance over a tiny bit of knowledge. The librarian, to his retroactive credit, can be said to have at least studied the matter to some degree, while Susan spoke more generally to a sense of justice. The Neustadt jury was, incidentally, international and partly Asian. The University of Oklahoma's great collection came into existence thanks to a touring oilman who bought every science book he could find in Europe after the First World War for the price of a small gusher.

In 1986 I offered LSU's archival library, Hill Memorial, my manuscript collection and my private library of small press, mostly poetry, books. The Hill's director at the time, Robert S. Martin, was happy to accept the donation. We negotiated the transfer of my personal library and that of my papers separately, for tax purposes. The books were tax-deductible, my personal papers were not. We understood the books to be the foundation for a small and independent presses' collection, beginning with the signed books that I'd kept since I started meeting poets in Detroit in 1966. I owned most of the books of my extended poetic family, a fertile community called variously "avantgarde" and "experimental" (funny-sounding words today when many of the participants are the new "mainstream"[73]). Hill Memorial promised to keep adding to the collection for as long as these poets continued publishing. My books constituted a fairly good picture of (more funny words) "the counterculture" or "the underground" of the late 1960s and 1970s. Hill had the books appraised by the Phoenix Book Shop in New York, a legendary place that specialized for years in buying books signed by poets in dire need of food. When I lived in New York I frequented the Phoenix a great deal. I was sure to find there my own books, signed to my "best friend" and I bought them back cheaply to give to my next "best friend," along with many other fine volumes of poetry dedicated to everybody's best friends by their best friends. The Phoenix owner's profit margin was small until the mid-1980s when many of the inscribed volumes became valuable. That time hadn't quite arrived yet, so the appraisal of my Hill Memorial donation by the Phoenix was modest. The tax deduction was small but Hill agreed, in addition to the deduction, to pay the printing costs for two issues of the (still) print journal I edited.

Some of my paper matter was inevitably lost during my moves, because it fell off trucks, dropped from shoulder bags, was lost in the mail on exploding planes, burnt for warmth in cold rooms, given away to drunks in generous

[73] "Mainstream," like "experimental," etc, are in quotes because there is no such thing, except in some kind of nostalgic recollection of a time when there was "order," when critics "ordered" the mess of what was being written. In practical terms, it just means "where the money is."

moments, lost in the snail-ways of the cumbersome zags of the old means of transport, and modified in unpredictable ways by climate. Storing my archive in an Archives was a comforting thought, but hardly the cure for the bad (good?) luck of being born at such a momentous time of transition between flesh and machine. Would any archive survive so much archiving? It remains to be seen. The crash of each of my hard drives was hard on me, made even worse by the certainty that a truly burnt drive can never be recovered, whereas for a lost notebook there is always the hope that thieves and time might return it.[74] One of my darker thoughts about the new technologies of storage and production is that they are designed to contain the record of the past (under the guise of preserving it) in order to destroy it.[75]

Even before I donated my paper mountain to LSU's Hill Memorial Library I was loathe to surrender my new work to e-memory, but I soon forgot, and almost without noticing I quit handwriting and typing on typewriters[76], and took to the new computer keyboards as if they'd always been there. All my records after the mid-Nineties were keyed in and logged into machines. Along with this went a kind of nouveau fatalism-

[74] A dim recollection: in 1974 I "xeroxed" five copies of my brand-new manuscript of short stories to take to Dennis Koran, my publisher at Panjandrum Press in San Francisco. I was in Berkeley and I stopped for a cappuccino at Caffe Mediterraneum on Telegraph Avenue, before heading across the bridge. While I waited for my cappuccino, somebody made off with my bag containing all five copies and the original. So confident was I of a happy ending, I'd destroyed all drafts and notes the day before. I searched every garbage can on Telegraph Avenue for the rest of the day. My reasoning: who'd want a bunch of paper when in possession of such a splendid hippie Peruvian wool shoulder bag? Alas. The stories never reappeared, the book was never published, and one of my masterworks is either still out there (dim hope) or it warmed up the homeless around an oil barrel fire (bright hope).

[75] This thought is so dark it is reprised several times in both text and footnotes. It would be interesting to use the exact same footnote to annotate different sections of the main text, but this experiment is for another time. Technically speaking, most poetry is fond of repetition, which varies with each reading, but being less trusting in this device, I prefer variations. The resolutely dark ("opaque") idea that computers store things in order to destroy them would cheer up archival librarians considerably: freed from the Info Cloud posed to bury them in a flash-flood any minute, they could return to the treasures in the monastic library and take up the proper job of a curator: defending text from the threat of time (which includes barbarians with torches and sweating cabbalists smudging text).

[76] My most productive typewriter was a Smith-Corona 220, mentioned in a poem so proud was I of it. My most triumphant was a Selectric ("with a ball") inherited from the LSU English Department office, when it acquired a computer. The Selectric didn't last long before my Kaypro 4 appeared, a "luggable" computer with a steel-blue casing made to look like something for use in an army bunker. The Kaypro used a machine language and two

(truly) floppy disks for word-processing: the actual word-program (WordStar) and the write-on disk; the machine had 36 k of memory, less than the cheapest watch now. The legend of the typewriter lasted for a century, first made famous by Mark Twain who dictated his autobiography to a "typewriter" (a human typist, as users of the machine were called, in what was possibly the first complete identification of a person with the tool). Twain's typewriter who took down his "autobiography" recalled in an essay that she tried to just type without listening to Twain who stood, arms behind his back, at a window, but he was so "funny," she said, that she would often burst out laughing. Clearly, Twain was playing to his young female "typewriter," which gives both his "autobiography" and his strict orders to keep it under lock and key for "one hundred years," a slight tint of rehearsed flirtation. William Carlos Williams devised a syllabic poetry form based on typewriter keystrokes for his publisher, James Laughlin, who was a poet but had no "ear," and needed a "measure." Williams gave him this melopeia by numbers, but here, too, one detects a touch of phlegmatic whimsy (and self-interest). Laughlin told this story delightedly many times, and his poems were not bad, but not because he counted the keystrokes. He was a genuinely talented lyricist. His modesty prevented him from taking himself too seriously, though he must have been bothered by this story, which shows both W.C. Williams and Ezra Pound (who started him in publishing) to be rather mercenary. American modernism (consisting largely of Pound and Laughlin's promotional efforts) can be easily described as a creation of the typewriter. The typewriter figures preeminently in satirical prose. On the occasion of discovering that Norman Mailer got $5/word for magazine articles, I wrote that every time Mailer heard that "click" of the carriage signaling the end of the line, he leaned back to have a cigarette: he'd just made another hundred bucks. Payment by the word was based on typewritten text, an innovation that favored popular magazine and genre writers. The best use of the creative ambiguity of the typewriter was made by my friend, poet David Franks (1945-2010), who used "correct-o-type," a strip of white paper used to lift typos off the page, to make slides from. In other words, he made film slides of his mistakes, which he then projected on a screen before audiences he lectured to about "typos." He used a pointer to focus on each slide of a mistake, and explain why the "mistake" or "typo" was significant. David's lectures were deadly serious, Freud would have approved of them; he developed a theory of mistakes as a language of the subconscious misdirecting the typing hand almost as authoritatively as a Ouija Board. Audiences were literally spellbound; they would have been even more astounded to know that in a very few years, months perhaps, typos would disappear and become quaint when SpellCheck rushed to correct all this involuntary language of (ostensibly) "mistakes." This Franks lecture might still be possibly found at ***poetdavidfranks.com*** (an interesting archival proposition in itself: the websites of those no longer among us, and their disposition: do such archives vanish or remain indefinitely in some nebulous corner of the internet?). SpellCheck blocked access to the secret language of typos, something poets understand, because the first thing the best of them do when they install a new Word program is to turn off SpellCheck. (Even so, the ease with which typing mistakes can be corrected on a computer has eliminated for all practical purposes the Language of Typos, which can now be capitalized like Biblical Hebrew or Sacred Sanskrit.) In the late Nineties of the last century, I took my friend David Weise, a computational linguist who was the chief developer of SpellCheck, to a Mardi Gras party in New Orleans at poet Lee Grue's house. David swore me to secrecy as to his creation and his job. He relaxed with a glass of wine in an armchair while poets, jazz musicians and assorted hipsters milled about talking shop and waiting for Lee's famous gumbo to be done. David may have relaxed a bit too much, because he suddenly overheard the words "SpellCheck" in the din of a babble about art. Even back then, in what was still the prehistory of computers, nobody was immune from the complications of the new technology. Once the dread compound noun had been spoken, David stiffened. I tried to redirect the conversation to something far from Microsoft, like the Fairy Parade that featured girls wearing feathers and nothing else, but it was too late. The congregation caught fire and proceeded to dissect and diss SpellCheck for all the offenses it committed against living language. David is a widely read man who could quote James Joyce to you, but he did nothing against this assault. Nobody had any idea who he was, but the topic stuck and was under attack until the gumbo was done. Lee's party was proof to David that there was no place he could hide, not even in carnival-crazed New Orleans among artists who smoke and drink. (In Seattle, where David lived, all those unruly customs and vices had been (mostly) purged.) The masque, the cigarette and the whiskey were no longer contraceptives against technology. The academic study of word-processing is trying to piece together a history and some hypotheses about the writing machines that are dictating the future, but I can't think of a better commentary than David's surprise at that party. Darren Wershler, the author of *The Iron Whim: A Fragmented History of Typewriting* (Cornell University Press, 2007), notes, "Writing about word processing when that's how you write is like trying to write about your own hand." Well, welcome to the 21st century. One of my friends, an eye doctor, told me in 1981 there are only two kinds of doctors who use the organs they operate on: eye and hand surgeons. It seems thinking about your hand while doing hand surgery would be a distraction, like postmodernism. Writers prefer their tools to be invisible, but the technology dictates the content whether the writer likes it or not. "Our writing tools are also working on our thoughts," Nietzsche typed, but McLuhan's message was starker: "the medium is the message." Time has proved McLuhan right, which explains a whole sideline of the archival enterprise, which is recovering early machine languages. Matthew G. Kirschenbaum, a professor of English and author of *Track Changes: A Literary History of Word Processing*, owns an Osborne, a Kaypro, a Tandy, an early TRS-80 laptop and an Apple IIe and IIc, and is fluent in the machine languages they used. He is also trying to discover who was the first novelist to use a word processor; according to him, it was most likely the science-fiction writer Frank Herbert, the author of *Dune*, who died in 1986; he submitted work to his publisher in the late 1970s on 8-inch floppy disks. The professor notes that Tom Clancy wrote his 1984 thriller *The Hunt for Red October* on an Apple IIe, using WordStar, making it the earliest word-processed bestseller, and Jimmy Carter set off what may have been the first word-processing-related panic in 1981, when he accidently deleted several pages of his memoir in progress by hitting the wrong keys on his brand-new $12,000 Lanier. I spent more time trying to figure WordStar on Kaypro 4 then I spent writing, and the result was certainly not a Tom Clancy bestseller, but a series of frustrated curses excoriating the technology. To the archivists' chagrin, writers were not thinking of preservation for the two decades when computers replaced typewriters, and few writers do even now, until they run into technical difficulties that drive them mad. Stephen King's 1983 short story *The Word Processor* (later retitled *Word Processor of the Gods*) captured the unsettling ghostliness of the new technology, which allowed writers to correct themselves without leaving even the faintest trace. In the story, a frustrated schoolteacher discovers by erasing sentences about his enemies he can delete them entirely from the universe and insert himself in their place, a reflection of Mr. King's fascination with his Wang System 5's "insert," "delete" and "execute" keys... "Writers are used to playing God, but suddenly now the metaphor was literal," Mr. Kirschenbaum writes. *The New York Times* article about his book notes Professor Kirschenbaum

*has received permission to use the corporate archive at Microsoft, where he hopes to trace the marketing rhetoric that helped create a near-mystical aura around a product designed primarily for the ordinary world of the office. ("More than words," promised one early slogan for Microsoft Word.) He also wants to pinpoint the beginnings of features now taken for granted, like spell-checking and track changes, not to mention the rise and fall of Clippy, the demonically cheerful animated paper-clip "helper" hatched by Microsoft in 1997 and subsequently killed off in numerous gleeful parodies.* (Jennifer Schuessler, *New York Times*, December 25, 2011)

You can add this anecdote to the second edition, professor.

optimism: if the machine destroyed my past it didn't mean that I had failed. Au contraire, it meant that I was a true poet, an anarchist, whose intentions were identical to the destructive movement of the machine. What was I conserving, when a "poet," as I saw it, was meant to create something "new" that saved only, if it saved anything, the misleading abilities of language? Destroying also, in the process of renewing, everything old and dated, including itself? Poetry pointed away from Archives to an Unarchive that stored possibilities and movement, not products. So why did I worry about my archive, a walking stick with worm tracks, that was, after all, only a display for a maze of traces leading to the unarchived unspeakable?

I hadn't always been fond of this inconsistency, but I slowly became infatuated. The fact is that humans have a self-preservation instinct, and that the most radical of us have more of it. A correction must manifest immediately, or there will be evil. Revolutionaries, from Robespierre to Lenin, compiled (or encouraged others to compile) manifestos, pamphlets and edicts as soon as the orgy of the revolution was over. Their less radical and even more fanatical followers saw to it that literature, monuments, museums and embalming[77] immortalized the radicals who overthrew the old order. Stalin's Soviet propaganda machine is an obvious example, but so is the Bibliothèque nationale in Paris, the largest archives in the world, which began with the revolutionary seizure of aristocratic and religious libraries in the French Revolution of 1848. The centralizing of Archives accelerated after the Enlightenment, as did increasing democratization, but the price for access was the loss of all history outside the ideology of centralization.

[77] The head of Lenin's embalmed body on view for eternity in Red Square in Moscow is stuffed with newspapers. How perfect! The head of a man like that, who made news for a century, is stuffed by the same newspapers he made news for, and they preserve this head, something one cannot say about the news in their pages. What do you call that? A papier-mâché archive?

Regionalism, marginality, subculture, orality were ejected by the centrifuge of centralizing Archives that retained only their amenable (attractive) expressions. Everything else became an Unarchive. The Unarchive that poetry pointed to was all the jagged stuff that the Archives rejected as it centralized knowledge. Poetry was useful only to a centrifugal history, an "Archives of Amnesia."[78]

In the posthuman age, the projections of revolutionaries, as well as the images of their revolutions, will be incorporated by the universal amnesiac flatness of the new archival technologies. The irregularities will be reabsorbed by the machines; there will no longer be a poetic project defending an Archives of Amnesia, because all of it, approved and unapproved history, will be just data. The machine will be holding all of humanity's memory hostage[79], and there will be no remembering without praying to the info clouds that will release their data rain in accordance to the accuracy of the prayers addressed to it.[80] After outsourcing our memories to the machines, the only mental possession we will be allowed to possess is an individual Password. This Password will allow an individual

[78] As per previous footnote, historiography has its own "underground" and "counterculture," historians who narrate the losers' side, the deliberate gaps in the winners' versions. These gaps are deliberately omitted by official historians, and less deliberately by the memories of those who were there but couldn't remember, so they took the official histories for their own. Amnesia has this weakness: it would rather stuff itself with the wrong stories than just stay empty. It's like an ulcerated stomach. Romanians say "better a broken sword over the fireplace than hanging from a beam." I know, it's an odd kind of wisdom, sometimes translated as "the sword doesn't sever a bowed head." Amnesiacs (losers and winners) have a thing about swords and heads: most of them would rather suffer a lie in their amnesia than a short sharp pain (as the amnesiac head rolls down the runway).

[79] Until the ransom is paid, a ransom that is equal to what is being held, which is to say that people must produce a virtuality as convincing as their history. And faster.

[80] A bit like the NSA is supposed to work: client agencies, such as the CIA and the FBI, must request specific information. The NSA was chartered to be neutral: to know everything but to release only what it considers specifically important to each request. In reality, the head of this uber-spy outfit is a political appointee who'll serve his patron.

94

access to various strata of the collective memory. The machine will release history, geography, genealogy, even complete films of one's life in real or compressed time (many of these will be used as obituaries embedded in tombstones, viewable to visitors from 9 am until 5 pm). This information will be available only to the extent that people will know how to ask for it.[81] In other words, the machines are streamlined by an ideology that resembles communism: to each what herm can handle and no more. The cloud, which is now just a remote server, will eventually become the whole sky, or, rather, the entire environment. In the end, all human brains will themselves become repositories of this common archives, but not necessarily of any history that concerns any particular (some)body. The human brain will serve simply as storage, like a locker, a bank box, but also interactive. These connected storage devices will be served by only those parts of the body useful to the collective Archives. In return, the Archives will release items of interest to the supplicant. At termination, everyone will become one's own tombstone, containing all the data herm asked for, but this lifelong data collective release is not free: the price is the body. Buckminster Fuller called humans "an information-gathering function," meaning that we evolved purposefully to be at the service of machines, doing what they want us to do. Many "useless" parts of the body are atrophying already as we reach our evolutionary goal: fingers, eyes, feet and reproductive organs will drop away as better sensory instruments fine-tune the brain. A future human will resemble a billiard ball filled with self-producing energy. But maybe we are these balls now, having projected our bodies out of an obscure yearning for esthetics. I won't speculate. At present, I

[81] Everyone will need access to databases because everyone will be an Archivist; the only job in the future is Archivist; archivists will be numbered by specialties: 1 for archeology, 2 for herbal medicine, 3 for subatomic physics, 4 for whatever.

don't yet feel fully posthuman, but my writing is a leap forward toward overthrowing memory for a posterity that may not need it, except as a backup, a manual of how to restore an image of "me" in case of a cosmic catastrophe.[82]

[82] Though it is hard to imagine a universe that is not a and post priori catastrophic, so that while one might imagine a human catastrophe, the background of its unfolding is an interactive indifference (or passivity) while catastrophe is an ongoing and constant (and thus imperceptible) mode. In the Cold War West, where a red cow drying up wouldn't raise as much as an eyebrow, other forms of shock took the place of that ideological slur. True, it was more difficult to shock and awe an audience in San Francisco after *Howl* was cleared of obscenity, and it became more and more difficult over the years after the standardizing of "creative writing" in MFA workshops, the assault on words by moving pictures and the reduction of language by the lazy babble of affluence, but real animals still find their way around the ongoing war on language, to provoke occasional conniptions (actually flying fur). The "official line" in the "capitalist West," as we used to call it, is that language is important only to the extent that it reveals official secrets. No one would think to denounce a poet for a verse, an attitude that is forcing true poets, more and more, to hack the websites of sinister government agencies and reveal their conspiracies through the poetry of the internet, before even turning it into iambic penthameter. An evident esthetic loss. At the time of my shocking teen assault on the Big Lie, the communists were not soft on dissenters: they prized language above everything else because their ideology was born of it. Words were currency, and poetry had high-denomination value. Capitalists weren't so sure: the post-war world economy was backing away from poetry, sensing obscurely that words were going to be put out of business by technology. (Actually they haven't: they merely became convertible into the universal language of Code and could be turned back into words like a reversible raincoat. The tower of Babel can be reconstructed and redestroyed by Code.) If I stray a bit from the archetype of the Sibiu Writers' Workshop, it is because the thread in the labyrinth that the creative mind must use to find its way out gets harder and harder to see. After the collapse of communism into the welcoming arms of consumerism, and the collapse of consumers into the welcoming arms of machines, came the collapse of language into the abyss of image-making, and then the collapse of humans into the blenders of hybridity.

Hybridity = inflation. Thus: my first published poem in *Flacăra* paid in *leis* what I like to think is the equivalent of $5 in 1963. My body of published work in Romania, twelve poems, brought in $60. I handed my mother this money, proud to be a bread winner. $60 was not inconsiderable: it bought a week's worth of tram tickets and potatoes. The poems of the poets I invented in 1967-68 were worth considerably more in my mind, but since nobody published them, they were worth nothing. On the other hand, gold was still $35/oz, and Nixon hadn't yet taken us off the gold standard. The redhead I was wooing at the Figaro must have read the deficit in my fierce gaze when she laughed. In 1970, my first book of poetry, written by three invented poets, brought me a $1,000 advance. The work of "invented poets" was already a hybrid form (me + the inventions) but 1970 dollars were already worth less than 1963 dollars by at least 20%. In 1974 *Poetry Magazine* in Chicago published a few poems I'd written expressly to fit in their lukewarm confines, and they paid me $1/line, for a total of about $300. The increased hybridity (writing for the format) corresponded to the inflating currency: in 1974 $300 was worth about one-hundred 1970 dollars. When my poems appeared in *Poetry*, my friend Ted Berrigan said, apropos of the $1/line payment: "Now write a thousand-line poem!" I didn't, unfortunately. In 2004 in Prague, Mary Carr said to Joseph Parisi, former editor of *Poetry* who had wrangled a two hundred-million dollar donation to the magazine from the Ruth Lilly pharmaceutical empire heiress, "How much do you guys pay now? Five hundred dollars a line?" Parisi laughed, but I don't think Mary was far off. $500 in 2004 were worth about $1 in 1970. (The hybridity sustaining *this* balloon was glaring: poets and drugs have always had a cozy relationship, but never in the history of the two products had there ever been any partnership between poetry and a pharmaceutical company!) The inflation started *racing* hybridity to get there. In 2011 when I visited, *Poetry* was already publishing prose poetry, and was paying staff to stare at computers in a new building that looks like an electric substation (a hybrid, that is, between the Parthenon and Chicago's famed steel-beam modernism). By the time *Exquisite Corpse* went online in 1996, the number of poetry submissions outnumbered possible readers by a factor of ten. Poetry-writing, aided by hybridity and inflation, had become a desirable occupation. The lack of readers introduced a new hybridity to poetry (verses sans lectors) and inflation followed. In my last year of teaching, 2009, I was obliged by the surplus to pay the poets in my class $5 for every poem they *didn't* write, like the US government paying farmers not to grow crops in order to keep prices stable. It cost me a pretty penny, but it didn't help very much. Prices kept falling: a 2006 poem was suddenly worth nothing, though a nonexistent poem (underwritten by me) was worth a mere $5, that is to say *almost* nothing. Poetry had become a perfect hybrid of words and dollars, and both things were worthless. Perfect inflation like perfect poetry was worth nothing minus what the author (or the author's patron) paid the potential reader to ignore what didn't exist. Two examples of such perfect hybridity are God and Facebook. Both of these entities are organized around a nonexistent object, and are composed only of followers. God is composed of believers, and Facebook is composed of its members. The richest companies in the world are ones who come closest to religion: they consist of a dense hybrid mass that labors in the name of a hollow core. By 2010 (when I officially terminated *Exquisite Corpse* because I was going bankrupt) poetry had acquired the dense mass of believers required, but it had become so hybrid it could not be told apart from either Facebook or the Catholic Church. It only took me fifty years to figure it out, the fifty years that it took poetry itself to create and solidify its hollow core. Another way to pose this creation of value ex nihilo and its disappearance into post-nihilo is that things out of context have no value, their value depends on their contexts. A thing can have many contexts with more or less value. Take something less abstract than poetry, a material tool, a knife for instance: lost behind a stove it is valueless; in a drawer its value is near zero, on a dinner table it is near-invaluable if the fare is gristly and tough; for sale in a window it's worth whatever its kind and make is selling for; plunged in the chest of a murder victim it is primary evidence. If it becomes a religion (the Knife in the Rock, let's say) its value grows immeasurably and then, just like the poem, it is stored and collected, but never seen. Thus, to use-value and surplus value you add archival value. And *faith*. If use-value has reduced this holy knife to dust, its archival value is only the memory of the knife. All things, poetry and knives, achieve an eventual reductio ad memoria, which is the value of their past existence. (And proof of it.) Memory is worth whatever the distribution of its simulations bring, it is the ultimate *thing*: The Thing-Without-the-Thing Archives.

The researcher, alone with herm ghosts in the damp underground Archives unreachable by bunker-busting bombs, must possess the faith of child-awe, and a myriad new skills to navigate the thick layers of erased vocabularies, only one of which is the breath-taking nerve of mid-20th-century poetry. We had it easy in those black & white days: the bipolar world I came of age in had decades to go before the fusing of plastic to everything that still held animal. A diligent researcher can, nonetheless, find anything, even the place where the Big Lie changed its language to sound almost like the non-thoughts of everyone else in the dis-curtained world. The creases, the seams, multiplied after the ideology of class utopia became the ideology of spectacle utopia. If the researcher can get that far, the difficulties should ease, until herm reaches the place where the outsourcing of human memory to machines begins exactly the thing minus the thing.

My papers, of course, didn't know what they were leaping forward to. This line of thinking wasn't yet born, certainly not yet articulated[83], when I actually donated my immense graphic hump. On the one hand, I thought that archivists would professionally revise the amateurish systems and stratagems of my Piler phase, and on the other I felt like I was giving myself up, surrendering, as it were, to institutional control. It baffled me that the word "library" meant both the public library and the archival library, two opposite aspects of a Janus-faced institution. I liked the public library for its overt eroticism. I enjoyed the sexual tension of strangers reading, barely containing themselves between carrels and shelves. To take out a book and find a pair of hungry eyes gazing from the other side of the shelf is a movie cliché, but what a lovely occurrence in real life! Urban public libraries are nests of perverts and, since they acquired computers, generators of porn. The erotic time/space of the public library is a world that deserves attention before vanishing readers and virtual books put out the wick. Giacomo Casanova, the 18th-century illuminist and libertine, wrote his memoir, *L'histoire de ma vie*, when he was librarian at Dux Castle near Prague. His patron, Count Waldenstein, possessed one of Europe's great libraries, composed in large part by books from monasteries abolished by the emperor. The Count's library was not public, but by framing Casanova's memories, it became the proto-public library. Casanova catalogued the looted monastic collections and remembered his sexy adventures. One sees the arrow of democracy here (Casanova's vertical plunge into his past) leaving the bow of the monastery for the opulence of the princely court, to head to the offices of modern architects making palaces for books available to

[83] Actually, it has been reached, by Marshall McLuhan and Buckminster Fuller, among others, and was already taken for granted in the Seventies, when a number of artists began projects for the disambiguation of archives, following other lines of thought, from memory traces inscribed in different ways on maps, bodies and buildings. Even the greatest believers in the similarity between human memory and machine memory will admit that they don't exactly know how human memory works. For a pre-computer vision of a mechanical analogy, see S. Freud's *The Mystic Pad*. (I almost wrote *Freud's iPad*, a different creature altogether.)

all. Ostensibly. It will be interesting to see what remains of public libraries, how their spaces will be reassigned, after books and readers are gone. I hope that they preserve their erotic charge by becoming sites for live performance and will continue housing the homeless, who will be the last ungooglable humans, and insofar as they will stay ungooglable they will provide continuity for performing the flesh body. Unless they become pool halls run by billiard balls.

The archival library is a different creature: its erotic charge is hidden; the stuff is shielded from view, to be seen only by researchers with backstage passes, like nightclubs catering to special tastes.[84] Maybe I was naive to think public libraries were even related to archival libraries, which are vaults, like the Federal Reserve, where narratives are adjusted to create the knowledge economy needed to turn out specialists. The open, slutty erotic aura of the public library was attractive

---

[84] There is probably a name for the syndrome of the archivist seized by the desire to destroy the holdings in herm charge. One of my favorite writers, J.J. Phillips, sent me an excerpt from a letter she wrote to her superiors at the University of Berkeley's Bancroft Library, an institution she has since left:

> *The function of libraries and manuscript repositories, and the work of librarians, archivists, and support staff is extremely important to humankind in countless ways, and is deserving of the utmost respect. However, while I know from direct experience just how thrilling and even magical it is to actually touch an ancient papyrus fragment or an old manuscript, or a famous writer's handwritten notes, it does not confer hieratic status on those who are so fortunate. Why a bunch of people imagine that they're inherently superior to others simply because they fuss over rare books and manuscripts, and get to touch and fondle these artifacts, and catalog information on famous writers (and occasionally rub shoulders with them) is beyond my comprehension. To me, this is nothing but textual fetishism, an exceedingly atavistic mentality. TBL, as far as I am concerned, is nothing but a fetish-house; a very big, very fancy, very wealthy fetish-house; but a fetish-house nonetheless. As I note in the enclosed letter, I came to TBL wanting only to do my job. I departed wanting to burn books... I love books. I love words. They are my lifeblood. So for such odium to be kindled in me – in a library with the most wonderful and fantastic books and papers imaginable, a place I would gladly get lost in (and frequently did), is a cause for great sadness.*

to me, while the Archives repelled me slightly, like an S&M club with rules and fetishes. My documents would eventually be digitized, but the physical objects would become more and more hidden, available for touch only to highly initiated super-perverts. I had good reason to ponder the eventual disposition of my oeuvre.[85] The virtual library has no erotic aura; paper documents, whether books or manuscripts, have been handled, touched, were in direct contact with human flesh; each time a book is borrowed and returned it acquires a measure of libidinal weight. A paperbookish culture is sexy: one-third of it is the weight of its libidinal substance. The virtual is forever virginal: it retains no sign of having been fondled (even e-annotated or e-underlined), it gives no hint of contact with human substance. When opening an old folder I am often overwhelmed by stale cigarette smoke, mine or others. Submissions to *Exquisite Corpse* often emanated a powerful whiff of tobacco that is more powerful the farther one goes back in the history of the magazine. Our 1983-1999 issues smell like New Orleans bars, the scent of cigarette smoke fades gradually after that, in tune with the masses quitting smoking, leaving only the hardcore, defiant to the end. Who was the last smoker to have submitted to *Exquisite Corpse*? A corpse now, he looks proud from wherever he is, at this distinction. Other signs of human use are feverish sweat, tears, sperm, blood—the liquids of bonding to words with the body revved up by them. In the age of cloning, we possess all we need to recreate our contributors in all their sensory effluvia, a huge neurotic capital that an archivist might unleash on the world one day as an aggressive act of retro art. Still, waiting for retro, I'd get impatient, even dead. At the moment, the only people in a position to

[85] Like the disposition of parts in the Romantic Era when body-parts of great men ended up far from each other in various reliquaries, I worry about a nouvelle vague of future archivists who might decide to reverse the classifications of knowledge by delegating pieces of a writer's work to the appropriate new categories, instead of keeping them integral. For instance, they might send all my poems using the Post Office metaphor to a newly created area of knowledge called "UPOM" (Using the Post Office Metaphorically), itself a subset of some grander division of the history of knowledge.

86 One of the founding stories of Romanians is that of young Master Builder Manole, the youngest of the three masons charged with building a princely church. Despite their best efforts, their walls crumble each day at dawn. One night Manole dreams that the walls will not stand until one of their wives is sacrificed by being built into the wall. He tells the others his dream, and they all agree that the first of their wives to bring them lunch next day will be immured. The two older masons tell their wives to stay home, but young Manole, who has just married and is greatly in love with his wife Ana, keeps to the pact. Ana arrives with his lunch. At first, she submits to having a few bricks and mortar set around her ankles, thinking it some kind of joke, but, as the building proceeds, she asks anxiously when the game will end. Manole does not answer. Tears run down his cheek, but he keeps stubbornly building his beloved into the wall until she is gone. The walls stand. When the church is finished, Manole leaps from the steeple into the turbulent waters of the Argeş River and drowns. On full moon nights one can hear Ana crying from inside the wall: "Why?" To that question, Romanians have been trying to give an answer throughout their entire literature. In the end, the answer may not require painful feminist introspection, but the simple moral that one shouldn't tell others his dreams no matter what churches crumble.

sniff our glorious human traces are librarians wearing white gloves (and nothing else) while licensed deviants train their genital probes on our remains.

This sort of thing didn't outweigh practical considerations. The books alone might have done me in. Just between 1970 and 1978 I could have been crushed to death by a million slim volumes of verse. Multiply that by one hundred after 1978. To prevent bibliodeath I gave away as many books as I could, keeping only what I thought I might reread, but even these privileged creatures were becoming menacing furniture. Static books are bricks: only when forbidden, or circulating, do they become lighter. I was being built inside a wall of books, like Ana, Master-Builder Manole's wife.[86] I had no time to read because I had to write more books to add another layer to my self-immuring. On the other hand, I looked at my books very much the way I look at a trash can: a good place to get rid of emotional and voluntary or involuntary injuries by writing and locking them in books. After disposing of them in this way, I felt renewed, revirginated, tabula erased and lighter, ready to acquire a new set of experiences, slights and wounds, and sufficient memories of them to pour into another book. In other words, the Archives was not just saving my body (from being book-crushed), but double-trashing the stuff by hiding it deeper. Of course, one might wonder why I didn't just burn the stuff, as many of my wiser colleagues have in the past, but I was obeying another obscure imperative here, the growl of a faithful retainer who bared herm fangs whenever my annihilating doppelganger showed up. Herm saved the stuff that Eros chucked to Thanatos by interposing herm (snarling archival) body between them. In addition to the equally matched Eros and Thanatos that share the body of every writer, there is this animal retainer who is either a blind worshipper or a prudent thief, like Ali Baba, the patron saint of Archives.[87]

If my books were deemed to have some tax-deduction value, my personal papers were a different story: in the eyes of the law they were valueless. I couldn't get a penny of tax advantage. The Authors League has been working for years to get a bill through Congress to make the donation of an author's papers tax-deductible. It hasn't happened yet. Even if this bill becomes law it will be too late: paper-holding authors will have become passé, and what's a cloud worth? Wordsworth had that one dead on: *"I wandered lonely as a cloud..."* How odd that my tender fate put me in the curve of the closing parenthesis of the print age! I often thought fondly about the hundreds of collaborations, letters, notes, and potential books in those taped boxes full of unfinished writings. I had planned to revisit them later, in that golden age of eminence when I had the luxury of time. There was so much more to be developed before it could be thrown away! "Later" never came, of course, and to an active writer it never does. A writer's "later" is a lot like "rereading:" often mentioned, rarely done. My papers as well as the major portion of my library in English went to Hill Memorial Library at LSU, and I donated my Romanian books and papers to the Slavic Library of the University of Illinois Urbana-Champaign.[88] I had found at last air-conditioned and friendly repositories for all the weight that had nearly crippled me in the years I'd carted it from city to city. The giant cockroaches known quaintly in Louisiana as "palmetto bugs" had already eaten through the binding glue of several taped boxes

[87] Ali Baba pillaged the treasure cave of the forty thieves by using the "Open Sesame" formula, but was cheated by his greedy brother Cassim, who did, however, get his comeuppance when he misspoke the formula and got himself locked in.

[88] Romanians, who hold that they are a people of Latin origin and speak a Romance language, are astonished that US universities always bundle them in "Slavic" studies. This is a political quarrel, intensified in the years of Soviet control, about the roots of Romanian; many words relating to agriculture and the Church are slavonic, and there is a Slavic word-double for almost every Latin word. Latinist and Slavic linguists clashed over this question for a century. In this respect, modern Romanian is the opposite of ancient Greek: instead of having two opposing meanings for every word, Romanian has two words for every meaning.

in my LSU basement office. The humidity in Louisiana made it impossible to maintain any paper document in a decent condition. I had reached that exasperated point in a long-lived writer's career when he finds himself evicted from his own house by the sheer mass of his products, which prevent him from understanding his own work, particularly the necessity to keep making more. Then there was the matter of the so-called "legacy" (the Ali Baba factor) which begins to gnaw at public figures (even anarchist writers!) around the age of sixty: what, if anything, did one do to ensure that one's creations would not be blown away by the winds of time like skiffs in a hurricane? (Nothing.) The creations were themselves designed to self-destruct: I considered a poem successful only if it had undone itself completely by the last line, like an unknotted knot or a Tinguely sculpture. The Escher drawing where it's impossible to tell which hand is drawing which was the blueprint for my works, followed in short order by the dripping acid that dissolved it, or the untied knot. Why, you may ask. Was there no educational, world-changing, idealistic agenda to a half-century of labor? Of course there was: the pleasure of making the thing. And the pleasure of seeing how it surprised people who were expecting the sheriff but were greeted by Echo and Psyche (nude) instead. How can surprise be archival? A poem in an archive loses its context, just as that same poem loses it in a predictable publication. The writer's job wasn't just making the thing, it was also creating the context in which the thing could do its magic. You can't make language without also making a "self" to house it in. That "self," the poem's context, is a mystery whose only job is to remain mysterious. The best work continues to surprise forever after it's written because it brings with it a new "self" every time it is read, a "self" that's none other than the reader's. The reader is modified by the poem to become its surprised context. Given this agenda, what exactly would my poems do in an archive except undo the Archives and the archivists. Among its other victims would be scholars who came to them with an a priori idea of what it is they might be encountering. These dangerous works of poetry are suicide-bombers who self-destruct on a pile of bodies. Who donates explosives to a university archives? A monster. The son of a printer and a minotaur.[89] In a mercenary vein, I kept hearing news of my less talented contemporaries selling (selling!) their private papers to university libraries or private collectors for considerable sums of money. These papers were not tax-deductible, but there was no law against selling them. This most reasonable reason had an ethical flaw: I was employed at LSU. It would have seemed (and would have probably been) unseemly to sell my papers to my employers; it might have looked like double-dipping. The University of Illinois Urbana-Champaign did not have any money to pay me, so I settled for the glory of being mentioned in their alumni magazine (not the first time I chose glory over cash, but that's another story[90]).

Robert Martin appreciated both the books and the personal material, and made it easy for me to transfer boxes from my apartment and office to the library building on campus. The contract we ended up signing called for periodical donations to the Library to add to the collections, an agreement that was originally some kind of boilerplate deed-of-gift that included not just my manuscripts but also the *copyrights*! That was tantamount to suicide, as well as the murder of my heirs,

[89] And a mythomane.

[90] See the story of the gold Roman coins in *The Life & Times of An Involuntary Genius*.

if they would have cared to renew copyright after the customary fifty years, so I struck that clause out. We signed this in 1986, several years before Google copied all the books in the world and made copyright as quaint an idea as a horse-wagon. At the time, however, it still seemed like ownership of one's work was a worthwhile goal. My relationship with Hill continued pleasantly through Martin's tenure, and to that of Faye Phillips who succeeded him. I felt reassured that I could access my materials as long as these folks guarded them. Additionally, I was assured that the technology of the Hill building would withstand an atomic blast. People may be gone, but my papers were safe! If the Martians cared to reconstruct the history of humanity from the vaults of Hill they'd be using my archive and that of Huey Long, their other great holding. Many writers I knew had sold or donated their papers to archival libraries, but we rarely discussed this, except as gossip if big money was involved. I may be wrong, or my case may be unusual, but a vague sense of shame hovered over the subject among my living friends. The dead, of course, talked about little else.

Being separated from the notebooks, drafts and manuscripts of my own work felt like I'd been wounded, had my flesh ripped, even if I hadn't taken a look at these things in years and often thought of them as refuse. They were a part of me, albeit a part that didn't often contemplate itself. Oh, who the hell cared? I decided to look only to the future. I donned my Carpe Diem persona.[91] There was always the hope that a future reader lurked there (at Hill) eager for the physical evidence. Someone who might see the scope of my lifelong project to give it the attention it deserved from a distance I

[91] I almost wrote "cape," which is better, of course, because it would cover the scars.

couldn't keep. This ideal critic with clear vision would be none other than a better myself in future bodies; the reason I had kept my notes, drafts, letters and napkins all those years was to make new literary works from them, works that lived for the brief moment before I decided what to keep and what to trash. Only a second of insight separated futurity from refuse, and the only impediment to realizing the work was time; between a note scribbled drunkenly one evening at the bar and the book that lived forever there stood a mere span of five years, my average for writing a book. My papers contained seeds that with five years' cultivation (per seed) would produce masterpieces. What I gave Hill Memorial were sacks full of seeds that some future myselves in a position to live, let's say, one thousand years, could turn into the literature of the future.[92] Since these myselves were physically impossible, I imagined them as perfect writer/scholar/philosophers who knew exactly what they saw when they saw it. Even just knowing the esthetic value of the paper seeds in Hill's keeping was worth it. Ah, metaphors! One can take them anywhere, they will always be an embarrassment. Still, all the time I was carting my journals, notes and napkins around I was certain that they'd become something larger than themselves one day.[93] That was, of course, before Internet killed Gutenberg, and made everything smaller, no matter how large it might have grown.[94]

Elaine Smyth, the new director at Hill, was a connoisseur of my kind of literature. I handed over to her what remained of my precious tonnage of creativity, and continued adding new material. I had managed to write in the original deed-of-gift the promise by the library of an eventual exhibition of materials from the collection:

[92] This amusing hyperbole will become painfully unnecessary when I realize (later in this essay) that everyone will carry one's entire archive within one's own body, and that the only way to think correctly about what one contains would be to apply a critical machine from outside the body and to bore laboriously into yourself, like a pick-axe-wielding Roman salt miner. This vision also contains my reply to the question "How do you know?" The answer to which is, "I just ask myself the question."

[93] Thanatos rolls his eyes: "Lawd!"

[94] A writer (or anybody's) creations are a mausoleum herm secretes like a snail until herm is but a microdot in a big house of bone.

a display of books, manuscripts, photos and letters so that my colleagues, who were not as well-versed in my oeuvre as Elaine, might see that a giant had dwelled inconspicuously among them. This exhibition, curated by Elaine, came to be in 2005, four years before I retired from teaching at LSU. It was a beautiful show. Elaine's curatorial insight into the documents of a half-century of literary activity brought me great satisfaction.[95]

The good feeling that came with this gratifying retrospective was temporary. After the show came down, I had second, third and fourth thoughts about making so much personal stuff available to strangers. One of my students wrote her graduate thesis on the work of my friend Kathy Acker, with whom in the early Seventies I'd had a correspondence and a friendship, called these days FB, Friends with Benefits. We took these benefits whenever there was an opportunity, but our connection was for the most part literary. When Kathy started mailing to her friends her notorious early novel, *The Childlike Life of Toulouse-Lautrec*, in serial monthly installments in brown paper wrappers, I wrote to her

[95] How weird is it to walk around with a wine glass in your hand (having it refilled often) at the opening of a show of your private papers and pictures? Weird, let me tell you. To watch strangers bend close to a glass case to inspect the spidery writing of a feverish nineteen-year-old writing in a language he didn't know... to see the mysterious smirk on the face of a classics professor whose eyes have just passed over a photo of yours truly in the photobooth at Molly's with a laughing topless German tourist... Ah, weirdnesses that unfolded private now public stuff, I should have noted you all and archived you myself, before Elaine got to them! The classics professor's gaze has just slipped from the photobooth photo to the longlimbed assistant professor with owlish glasses who he just hired but could have married if they had been hired at the same time in another century, but impossible now of course, twenty years after he married the first assistant professor he hired, his second wife after the fellow graduate student he married, who is now a full professor married to a graduate student, sigh, and then his gaze slips back to the inside of the photobooth at Molly's where his colleague is fondling the perfect left breast of a girl so beautiful he cannot imagine her wearing those owlish glasses, though with a little adjustment, a longer skirt, a classics education... sigh again. Move on to the next picture: his colleague is smiling with his arm around the tall, sturdy ninety-year-old poet Aimé Césaire in Fort-De-France, Martinique... Césaire is smiling too, at the photographer, who is Laura, wearing a short skirt the nonagenarian is unabashedly smiling at... but the professor does not see Laura's skirt, he sees only history... (Note to this note: if you hear a writer whining that herm novel is stalled, don't believe it. The novel's going on without the writer.)

asking what she thought she was doing. It was an innocent question, influenced in no way by the fact that
our mutual friend J, as well as myself, were characters
in that strange confection. I received back a six-page
handwritten-in-pencil letter from Kathy, explaining
and defending her method. This was the only time in
my knowledge that Kathy came close to revealing any
personal esthetic, so it was doubtlessly of interest to a
young scholar. Kathy passed away, so this may indeed
be the only "theory" she wrote about her work. My
student did find the letter in the Hill Memorial archive.
"Was it useful to you?" I asked her. She gave me a quiz-
zical look. I was baffled: "Didn't you find it interesting?" "It's not that," she said, "After Kathy explained
all sorts of literary things, she added a post-script..."
"What was it?" "Well, it said, 'if you come to the city
and don't fuck me, I'll kill you!'" We had a good laugh
over that one. This post-scriptum did not contradict
in any way either Kathy's esthetic or the tenor of our
friendship. But the whole thing did give me pause.
How many of these kinds of things, a lot less apropos
or even appropriate, lay among the hundreds of artifacts I'd handed over? It had been only Elaine Smyth's
good sense to make the exhibition as tasteful as it had
been. If she'd been out to make me into a monster,
she could have doubtlessly done it. The presence of my
private papers in a library, available to scholars of every
kind—good, bad, indifferent, malevolent, etc—was no
laughing matter. How many people had I offended wit-
tingly and unwittingly in thirty years of publishing a
pugnacious and polemical literary journal? Or ridiculed
privately in letters I'd never re-read? And how many of
those offended people were now comfortably settling
into tenure, professorships, grant committees, and art

bureaucracies? Oy. I suddenly had the vision of a legion of army ants in doctoral robes descending on my collection with poisoned dart guns. There went the future of my literary reputation! My sacks of seeds weren't sprouting! They were being eaten by rats! I mean ants.

At a used bookstore in Kansas City I bought a biography of Kay Boyle by Joan Mellen. I'd met Kay briefly in the Seventies in San Francisco, and I admired her writing, her fortitude, her radical views. From the very first, Mellen's well-documented biography started feeling like a vendetta, and I asked myself why and for what reason would anyone write a hostile biography of anyone, given the huge amount of work involved. I then realized that the author was probably writing her own autobiography under the cover of Kay Boyle's biography. One of the consistent themes of the book was how beastly Kay had apparently been to her children. Doing the math, I figured that the author was close to the ages of Kay's children or grandchildren and that she might have been working out her own oedipal conflicts via her subject. It was a chilling thought, but a familiar one. Ed Sanders had once warned that the hostile biographies won't be long in coming for any of us. Edgar Allan Poe was hardly cold in his grave, Ed said, when two hostile biographies appeared. Hard to know why. Someone's morality might have been offended by Poe's child bride cousin. The other might have hated his poetry, or met him at a party where Poe had insulted him. Who knows why a scholar or even a non-scholar would undertake a time-consuming, years-long work for the purpose of doing a writer in? Jealousy, frustrated ambitions, slights are as good as any other reasons. My future readers, instead of being my ideal self-substitutes, were more likely to be my ideal nemeses. Of course I reminded myself that in these days of instant celebrity, when the subject of a biography or a biopic is born simultaneously with his or her biography or biopic, and that sometimes the biography is even born *before* its subject, *vide* fictional people on Facebook, it's hardly worth worrying about a posterity that is, like books, already passé. By the time anyone gets to my stuff, my scandals may be afterschool family fare, G-rated, and hardly worth a shudder. I do miss the 20th century. The second half, anyway. Au fond, aren't all writers' biographies hostile? The form itself is implicitly a recognition that there exists an alt-story, an alternative life that the author's work does not tell. This life—extractable from notes, marginalia, correspondence, witnesses, family—can and often is put in the correct order (chronological or otherwise) by the biographer. The deeper the researcher digs the more evident it becomes that the literary, recognized work for which the author gained recognition, is in fact an elaborate *coverup*. The literature was a means of hiding the true life that can now be reconstructed from studying the unguarded material. So even if a biographer begins with the intention of writing a "sympathetic biography" (a near oxymoron) herm ends up by uncovering in the archive the story that the author went to great (literary) lengths to conceal. The biographer, who has by now spent over a decade pondering scribbles in illegible handwriting, evidence of secret affairs, craven compromises and innumerable instances of weakness and guilt, will now begin to feel less than friendly toward the subject. Some, like Joan Mellen perhaps, become positively furious with their (former) heroine. They feel betrayed. They have spent precious time getting to know an enemy. They could have created

96 Or gets wiser and begins herm next job as a literary critic instead of a biographer, sacrificing readers to the cause of uncovering the crime that is surely there wherever writing is committed. There is a biographers' hierarchy of difficulty, as well as a hierarchy of freedom; on the shallow bottom of difficulty are noncanonical poet-subjects: their biographers have to write prose but needn't worry excessively about a crowd of junior biographers jostling to undo or redo their work; the biographers of little-known novelists have to work harder because they must try not to sound like the authors they are writing about, an effort that begins to show on page two; the most difficult job is that of the biographers of autobiographers who must disbelieve everything an autobiographer has said about hermself, which means going mano a mano with a ghost. (The difficulties increase depending on whether they are dealing with a prolific or an elliptic ghost.) The hierarchy of freedom applies only to biographers of historical and political figures, or nonverbal artists, dancers, musicians, scientific minds and/or freaks. The biographers of historical/political figures have the least trouble: they can create their figure from research, certain that they are taking their place in an ongoing inquiry that is as good as they can make it: their research is more important than their style, and accuracy is more important than passion (though it helps). Biographers of artists, dancers, musicians, scientists and oddballs have nearly the freedom of something themselves instead, a shiny literary cover just as elaborate and grand as the one their subject had. The coverup they had uncovered could have been theirs if only they'd realized sooner that their own crimes deserved a majestic coverup. Perhaps the writer under scrutiny has done nothing wrong, maybe there is no crime, though there is clearly a coverup. Maybe the criminal is the biographer, thinks the biographer to hermself, invading the privacy of a defenseless corpse, violating it with herm prose? Perhaps, thinks the horrified biographer, the crime of living prosaically is the only crime. Sure, a very good novelist may be covering up the crimes of an entire community, may in fact be a Christ of Fiction, and a good biographer can expose what lies under Tolstoy's vast canvas, for instance, and become in that sense a character in the epic, a hero even, a writer who displaces the author of the coverup, an iconoclast, a deicide. Who can blame the biographer who, five years into intense research, finds hermself cheated by fate, a fate no other than herm altruistic-modesty-cum-hero-worship turning into dismay and resentment? The only crime is the theft of innocence. Somebody must pay, and it has to be the dead author. Biographers learn from the authors they study what the techniques are, exactly, for turning life/lives into myth. These techniques are of no use to them, alas, by the time they discover them, because now they know both sides of the coin: the imaginary and the real; it takes all the fun out of the adventure of creating one's self (or a self for one). The imaginary that looked real enough to chain them to the archive, turns out to have been a misguided impulse that led them, sadly, to reality. The poor scholar, the sad archive rat, now hangs himself in a novel by Bohumil Harabal.[96]

Writers have always known that personal papers, drafts and correspondence are dangerous. Mark Twain put a hundred-year lock on his own "autobiography," an excess of caution, really, since he was so prolific it has taken a hundred years just to publish his unlocked work. Some of it, like his savaging of Mormonism, will always be writing non grata in Utah. Writers less prolific

imaginative writers; there is research, yes, but there is also the freedom of exploring with words the ways of brain and senses that do not primarily use words to express themselves. The nonverbal subjects can even be an accessory to the uncovering of their expressions by the biographer. And then there is the complete freedom to write granted to the biographers of imaginary authors. These biographers are authors in drag; their only "crime" is a misdemeanor: to cover up the fact that they invented their subjects. Graduate students, who have (or think they have) time, do not write biographies: they write theory. The price for writing theory is steep: outside of their graduate committee, they will have few readers: writing theory means literally "sacrificing readers to God": there are one thousand more readers for a biography than witnesses to the slaughter of their own intelligence; that is, an essay has three readers (masochists) for three thousand readers of a biography (sadists). As noted before, biographies without subjects are the freest form of textual interest, so the path is open to the enterprising biographer of a nonexistent subject; this type of "biography" is also a work of criticism/theory, so a critic who wants to be read must call herm study "biography." Writing the biographies of fictional personages makes the biographer a critic and a novelist who is in a position to uncover the crime of herm subject at leisure, retroactively. My made-up poets may have been written in order to discover their crimes in the process of writing them. The tantalizing aspect of producing imaginary people is being a good enough detective to find out what crimes their words cover. The archives of imaginary people are themselves fictions, so there is the added bonus of (re)searching whatever catches the author's eye or ear. Floating between these forms of essaying is both the most and least difficult, the freest and the most contained: the Biography of A Thing. How can a thing that is not "alive" have a *bio*? Simple: all things have life in them, a life that can be researched and scribed without reference to its history or "meaning." There isn't a lifeless thing in our universe: this I know. Take the thing we most often discuss here: a book. The biography of a book, any book, as a thing, an object made of paper and words: the biographer of this thing must begin in the prehistory of the writing surface and the origin of writing, perhaps decipher linear A. The content is only of slight importance, freeing the biographer to imagine the object from its beginning in clay on cuneiform to its disposition as a brick in a future house made of books. How to speak of a book as an object, without discussing its contents, might be difficult for the reader of this book to imagine, so let's take the wheel of a Ford Focus 2012: The history of this automobile's wheel is no less liberating and constraining than the history of the book: it only matters where the biographer begins. If the biographer of the wheel needs to reinvent it, so be it. The biography of a thing liberates the researcher from all other things, it gives herm a claim of immunity; herm is released from the guilt of feeling any impingement on one's writing self. The blameless self of a thing's biographer absolves writing itself from the guilt of not being a *thing*. There is such a thing as writing, but writing is not a thing—unless it is the biography of a thing. Whatever disappears in the act of being used cannot be said to be a *thing*. A *thing* is that which remains itself while in use. To say of writing poems, "I'm making things," like Ted Berrigan used to, is to assign them the wishful solidity of doors.

than Twain do have reasons to worry, so it may be a good idea (for nonfiction writers especially) to time-encapsulate some stuff that still threatens. Literary writers can afford to be even more radical. Gogol burned the sequel to *Dead Souls*, which he'd written after his religious conversion, a gesture Nabokov called "one of the most charitable acts in Russian literature" (the burning, not the conversion). Archives librarians have to be the attentive angels in charge of a writers' papers; they have to be part censors, part protectors, part benefactors (to researchers), and part perverts (in the noble sense of loving their charges a bit excessively). They cannot burn what the living author failed to, but they know what herm should have. Archivists are angels in charge of an author's afterlife: a flick of the wing and they can either disperse it to the winds or whoosh it into the right hands; they stand with feathers, not matches, between an author and the vultures who want the author's remains. Judging the intentions of a vulture is a tough job. Until proven otherwise, I'd assume that every researcher is a starving vulture pretending to be a poor library mouse. The armed angel takes no sides, but herm may be no angel at all, but a spider, weaving herm own autobiography from the papers in herm keeping. Or, since we are in the animal world, the archivist may be a dirt-dauber who deposits the scrolly spiders of my papers and rolls them into herm nest to devour at leisure. My ideal job, I sometimes thought, would be to care for Edgar Allan Poe's papers at the Enoch-Pratt Library in Baltimore. My corner office would look over the autumnal Peabody Square at the statue of George Washington, while I dreamed myself a life from the unfinished hints in Poe's notes. My own life would be hardly worth noting: in the morning walk to work at the Pratt, a mere three blocks across the leafy square from my one-room bachelor pad on the tenth floor in the building housing the American Psychoanalytical Society where Sigmund Freud delivered his first lecture in America; go to lunch at the pub where H.L. Mencken once held court; dream away the afternoon over a first draft of *The Masque of Red Death*; make distracted comments in notebook; after work have drinks at the Peabody Hotel with the attractive Walters' Gallery curator who is way too young for me; at closing time pour her drunk into a taxi; return to my pad; dream of her. Leaves keep falling, la vida es sueño.

Lost objects slumber like vampires until activated by some fluke. Every archive contains numerous such dormant creatures waiting to be activated by the right circumstance. The Renata Pescanti Botti book-cum-Codrescu-notebook slumbered with an eye open for David Faulds, who aroused the vampire. David's act may in fact stand for the whole archival mission: to help sleeping artifacts to wake by matching them at the right time to the right person (though not always to the best effect). An angelic job, this. Put that wing down, David.[97] Our present zeitgeist doesn't need Archives any more than it needs books, so being an archivist-angel is no picnic. I'm not flattering anybody here.[98]

[97] Fluke and Fauld (*fluke*, chance, luck, a broad triangular plate on the arm of an anchor, either of the lobes of a whale's tail, *fold*, cattle fold, pen, surrender ((*fold*)) crack in the earth, or a wrong action ((*fault*))). A book with fault surrenders by chance to an anchor released by David Fauld.

[98] My return to Romania after almost three decades was rewarded with the prizes due a prodigal son: barbecued goat, beautiful young journalists, brilliant translators, residencies at the Black Sea (where Ovid pined for Rome), and a Legion d'Honneur-type-distinction. I was among Romania's first exiles to return, to cover the 1989 revolution that toppled the tyrant whose laws had prevented me from returning. In other words, I definitely went "home" again, but only as a form of revenge against Augustus Cesar. Unfortunately, Cesar died before he pardoned Ovid, who lived past even the death of the next emperor, Tiberius, who either forgot him, or no longer received Tristae from Ovid, who resigned himself to his exile. Not my fate. I did have a list of public deeds that made being born in Romania worth rewarding, so I had no reason to feel the guilt that causes Europeans to reward minorities to show how terrible they feel about colonialism and Jews. Had I done nothing but be Jewish, I would not have been rewarded in Romania, however, because Romania only felt esthetically, not politically, European, even after it officially joined the EU. After that, it was permitted official hypocrisy. Not to diminish the discernment of my honorable partisans, there were plenty of grimaces in the mass of smiles greeting my "triumphal return." From 1989 until 1995, Romanians struggled with language: they did their best to elevate public discourse to reflect the mood of the street without using the vulgate; they eliminated from the media the empty words of the communist era, such as "comrade," "solidarity," "workers' state," "the new man," etc, the hollow rhetoric that monkeyed Soviet dictums. It wasn't easy: the word "comrade" still sounded more natural than "mister" for many years; "kike" (*jidan*) more organic than "Jewish" (*evreu*), but eventually communist-era

speech was denatured, and new slang and media-language appeared. After dealing with language, the best minds started working on erasing the historically-rooted meanings of the disappeared words, a much harder job, but necessary if Romania was going to be truly accepted into NATO and the European Union. How much it succeeded is debatable. The war in Yugoslavia made all the old Soviet-controlled areas wary of making too much of their national pride, which resided in large part in the meanings eliminated by EU requirements. Now (in 2012) the fiction of the European Union is unraveling and the old meanings (without

Sad plight of the archivist aside, what does the existence of a writer's private papers mean to *literature*? A lot, as I realized at the Lockwood Memorial Library at the State University of New York in Buffalo. I was shown a slim schoolboy's notebook with every line underlined, later expanded to flow into something called *Ulysses*. This schoolboy's notebook had been the tiny spring from which the 20th century's greatest novel had flowed forth. I shook off nostalgia. The 20th century didn't miss *me*. The Archives was lucky to have this item, and would have been so even if its owner hadn't gone back to it, like Joyce had; even at the risk of serving to disappoint scholars, or the even greater risk of serving as the

words) are re-emerging. Aleš Debeljak makes the point in an essay on "Slovenia's path to the EU" by describing the emptiness of EU's chief symbol:

> *Little affection is prompted by euros... The design had to please many constituencies and is of course a result of a compromise. Is the euro banknote a mirror of Europe and Europeanism? Consider: what visually distinguishes the €5 bill is an image of a vaguely ancient viaduct that could have been erected anywhere in the former Roman Empire. The €10 bill shows what looks like a Romanesque portal while the €200 bill bears an opaque glass door and a kind of iron bridge. The euro is unlike various national currencies, in that it is too timid to show a face and too reticent to suggest a biography, to give pride of place to a story. Not a single human being appears on these banknotes. Incapable of inspiring any meaningful identification and failing to deliver on the imperative de te fabula narratur, these banknotes are abstractions. In vain one searches for portraits of such familiar figures as Erasmus, Shakespeare, Michelangelo, Mickiewcz, Velasquez, Newton, Goethe, Andrić. The columns and arches on these notes instead suggest ruined empires, transformed into a longing for connection and community. They resignedly echo something lost in the sands of the irrecoverable past with no foundation and no recognizable landscape. In other words: the iconography of euro banknotes represents a no-man's land, bereft of history and memory. Must we sadly infer that contemporary Europe is a land with no founding events, heroes, or battle for independence? Is it soon to be without its currency too? (EU newsletter, December 20, 1989)*

Debeljak has nailed it: the national stories, the "meaning" of behaviors and even physiognomies of the diverse people of the EU, have no place to go in the "union," even if they are, in the first place, kitschy affairs of past sentimental narratives. What is the archives of the EU? A collection of bureaucratic documents intended to erase the violent passions of its members, while replacing them with the pallid simulacra of culture. My home town, Sibiu, named by Forbes as "the eighth most idyllic place to live in the world," is a UNESCO " cultural treasure." I remember it fondly as the locus of my unhappy childhood.

basis for hostile biographies, a notebook might contain *in nuce* a great novel, and thus a warning to all future researchers: self-distortions are temporary, the material remains unchanged, its uses are multifarious in an unpredictable future. This *material* is, for all practical purposes, *the end*.[99]

In the e-era, paper documents will be held in secret safe rooms, like those in medieval monasteries, available only to special "clean machines" and, at a high price, to the super-perverts, who are wannabe machines[100]. The "clean machines" will themselves be assembled by machines assembled by machines, a process that will begin with specialized humans working separately on different sections of assembling machines. Paper from the past will be accessible to the uninitiated only via an unbreakable Da Vinci Code. The initiated will be a few top preservationists—their job will be strictly technical, making sure the artifacts don't disintegrate. Digital libraries (the clouds) will be more malleable, easier to use, more responsive to researchers, but always and only digital. If a human hacker with animal intentions breaks the code to the room holding the paper documents, the machine will eliminate the human, then self-destruct. The paper documents, if they predate digitization, will be in great demand, a desideratum-canthavum; every researcher will want to *feel* the trembling hand; it will be tantalizingly close in the e-maze of the (possibly) solid architecture of the perpetuum-mobile building, but never more than "close." The handling of material touched by a poet will be out of reach for the sensualist researcher who likes to palpate, sniff and count strikethroughs. Of course, such sensual researchers are rare, since critical exegesis is performed mostly

[99] Unless it dematerializes: I saw a shoebox in the same Archives, containing the manuscript of William Carlos William's novel *Farmers' Daughters*, written on cheap paper given to Dr. Williams in exchange for some medical favor, the manuscript poofed into a cloud of flakes every time the box was opened; the manual typewriter Williams used punched holes in the cheap paper; the novel evanesced out of these holes. The box wasn't opened often: I was a special guest. And a party to the crime of the manuscript's disappearance.

[100] Super-perverts are understood here to be the most rule-bound humans in existence, hungry for post-humanity, in a hurry to become as perfect and feeling-neutral as machines. Super-perverts are kept back from joining the machines only by the pleasure they feel in machine-like activities. Pleasure, obtained in whatever way, is still eminently human.

[101] Who would be surprised if a number of Shakespeares were typing madly in some illegal laboratory, trying to produce monkey text?

[102] This may be our landscape already; the number of significant viewable original documents is diminishing rapidly. If you have visited an antique bookshop lately, you will doubtlessly notice a precipitous drop in the availability of old books and manuscripts. Even junk stores no longer sell junk made before the advent of plastic Japanese toys. Collectors are driven by an obscure and powerful urge to acquire every non-virtual object. Objects are disappearing as fast as it takes virtuality to become more realistic (that is to say, milliseconds). And then 3-D printers will produce objects indistinguishable from what disappeared.

[103] It is to be hoped that the "clean machine" will be unable to separate intention from production, setting up instead indiscriminate channels that broadcast the entirety of a writer's archive without judgement. The "All Codrescu All The Time" channel will be always be on, on a loop, and, since it will only be one of jillions (all sign-making humans will have such a channel) it is up to human researchers just how much to resent and how much to love. Their sentiments will be added to the broadcast.

[104] Another circular image: the coffee cup stain, the armpit sweat on shirt, Philip Roth.

on printed text, that older virtual medium. A writer's archive of unpublished material is also used mainly for the intellectual information therein, though in the case of a few classics, the condition of the manuscripts, the grain of paper, and the author's drops of sweat on the page are important as well. Sophisticated analyses of the physical oddities of documents can lead in all kinds of directions, including the physical replication of the author through the genetic information contained in the sweat.[101] Mostly however, under the weight of critical consideration of virtualities, the imperfections where the poetry resides evanesce. Since my poetry resides entirely in the imperfections of my body, it will evanesce. Maybe not a great tragedy, but my poetry isn't the only one to spring twisted from ink-smudged paradoxes. What about William Blake? Critical work derived from digital copies will become even more bountiful, but no poetry will survive it. In fact, critical work itself won't survive; exegesis will die along with what it tried to exegise. The machines will transmit perfect copies via clouds to the researcher, but the original documents will never be seen, and there will be no proof that they exist. The de facto infoscape of the near future, 2015, let's say (generously)[102], will be foregrounded perfection on a background of suspicion. Reader, you can be the last human to touch my papers. Hurry![103] Digitally-derived critical work will be itself digital, so it will be only an addition to the ongoing imperial virtuality. Commentary excises the circular ring of the sweat drop on the manuscript page if it isn't sensually verifiable. The exegesis already contains both the content of the object it observes and its view of it. In the absence of the human stain[104] the studious internaut will be equipped with projections that float forever in digital symmetry. Material dirt, that is to say non-digital dirt, will be a secret currency, the "gold" that guarantees the ongoing existence of human beings.[105] The digital drains the body from the text, that is to say it deprives the text of its gravity by stealing its dirt, the sweat, tears, sperm, blood, gooey sentiment, found junk, folk carving, craving for sugar; it replaces the gravity of random traces with information reduced to (perfect) code.[106]

My posthumous career (rush urgently to Hill and U of I now[107]) will be like every other writer's in the coming virtuality, with the proviso that every

[105] J.J. Phillips, who'd cared for novelist Richard Brautigan's papers at the Bancroft Library, comments:

*I know you know that Brautigan blew his brains out, literally blew his mind. What you might not be aware of is that he blew his brains out all over pages of his last manuscript. I've handled them, archived them, touched his brain matter on numerous occasions, though at first I had no idea what I was touching because TBL said nothing and even denied what became all too apparent after I eliminated the other possibilities of what this strange stuff could be (I'm not unfamiliar with such things, and my eyes didn't deceive me). I see what's on these pages as something of a completely different order than coffee stains, cigarette burns, the tomato seeds that Josephine Miles idly spat onto her mss., even drops of spit, blood, semen, boogers, and the like. With Brautigan, these are the actual physical remnants of brain tissue, blood splatters, and cerebral fluid of the very brain that created the ideas he had and the words he wrote, now creating its own narrative on top of those words; and of course that act insured he'd never think or write another word. Those pages constitute both a palimpsest and something incomprehensibly more. The two 'expressive' mediums, the mingling of flesh and word made flesh, merge into one unbelievably complex and believably simple text of death.*

This violent trace complicates the matter, indeed, not just because Brautigan knew that he was destroying the possibility of any future archive of his never-to-be-work, but because the archivist herself is touched by the corporeal violence of the suicide. J.J. can and possibly will write her own archivist's memoir (she has written a poem, *Brautigan's Brains*, see corpse.org), but I wonder if another side of the argument for (or against) the digital does not rest *entirely* with the keepers of the archives, who are, as noted many times in this essay, not just keepers of remains and executors of wills, but also judges and forensic analysts; possibly, *final* judges and *last* signatories of analyses. If this is the case, the Archives loom as a much larger threat to the culture Brautigan sought to escape, than even the endless reproduction of digitization.

[106] Code replaces language, Babel falls; like a reversible raincoat code can turn back into language, but it's language that knows it's code underneath. What's lost: the human inside. What's gained: protection against rain, against fertility. This raincoat is a condom that consumes its wearer by stripping away babel (babble, rubble). The language side of the reversible condom is merely decorative: code keeps it for sartorial hubris, to remind itself of the time before its revelation, like the sniper who keeps a dartgun on the mantel piece. The walls are one smooth nuke.

[107] Addresses and contact numbers provided on request, andrei@corpse.org.

career that begins now will be posthumous. Most of my work was made in the flawed past, but the new poets will begin ahead of themselves, in a body-less future. Some of them will still feel, for a short while, the human vacancy, but such sensitives will be seen by their less sentimental contemporaries as counterproductive nostalgists, just like we modernists regarded romantics in the 20th century. Cranks and fools!

At the end of the 20th century, I remember the liberating joy of writing a smart, mad, instantly revisable letter by typing directly into an email, in response to a mad, beautiful prose epistle from Tom Robbins, great American novelist. I remember printing out his letter, but not mine. His was still surrounded by the golden aura of writing as a sacramental-scriptural act. (I hoped, of course, that he would print out my response because, instant as it was, I thought of it nonetheless as *mine*, not *mine and the computer's*!) As the era of the email letter became our de facto means of communication, I remained, for a time, aware of the difference between what I still called an "epistolary exchange," with eminences like Tom Robbins and Willis Barnstone, for instance, and the rest of my communications. I conscientiously printed out the "important" letters to keep in separate folders, just as I had in the days of snail-mail. I never printed out my own letters, still convinced that the other side would take care of it. As I became more trusting of the new medium I quit printing *any* letters; clearly, the hard drive kept them all in its memory as safely as the bank held my money (joke). A few lost and irrecoverable hard drives later, I felt as miserable as I did when I lost my first notebook. Gone forever my digitalized uniquenesses! Had I but backed them up! I switched to Gmail when it was first introduced, an entity whose server, unlike my personal drives, preserved all that I sent and received, an infinite repository guaranteed by the faith of millions (just like the Federal Reserve). Correspondence with other than "eminences" became perfunctory, however: no form of address, no pleasant closing conventions, rarely a signature; lots of information, plenty of business, hasty opinions; things that wouldn't have merited a stamped letter or even a postcard in the old days. Gmail kept everything, the brilliant prose of "eminences" along with the back-and-forth with the car service for my next gig; it relieved me of any need to be selective, careful, *archival*: by preserving everything, it offered future scholars/biographers practically infinite possibilities of interpretation and consideration. Or so I thought, in that fraction of time after the Big G-Bang. Of course, such archival wealth would also require an infinite number of future scholars/biographers and an infinite number of humanities programs to produce them. And if these scholars/biographers are none other than my future selves (since I can't admit my enemies into this crowd), let's just get down to business and clone a few thousand of me, like a modest first printing. On the other hand, if every word has been automatically archived by the G-Great Server, each word is a seed of myself and I am therefore not just immortal but the only One. Hold the cloning. Gmail has collapsed past, present and future into a single solipsistic entity, an infinite hall of mirrors. The archival library (the building, the paper, the materials) ceased to matter after G-D, the Great Digitizer, came to earth and *flattened* everything. Imperfection no longer existed in the e-archived future, because imperfection (the trembling hand, the erasure, the typo, the half-burnt page) disappeared, leaving, if anything, only a perfect image of itself. The e-archived repository will have researchers but no heirs, if one understands by "heir" the type of researcher/scholar/writer who continues the work by highlighting its flaws, its imperfections, its aborted dimensions. An "heir" inherits (hopefully) in order to continue, but if there are no palpable imperfections, there is nothing to continue *from*. If my only heir is a clone of myself, and an immortal one at that, there is no future. There is no point in visiting an Archives that is its own perfect record: both "I," once-and-forever producer, and the archived product inhabit an eternally flat present.[108] The "clean machine" washes its hands (again). What followed the archiving of self-production (the Age of Google) was even more phenomenal: Facebook. The Age of Social Networking now collected not just the archive of a lone self, but also the self in society, the actions of self in relation to other selves, and thus became an Active Archives. If the Cloud in the Google Age was filled to bursting with the authored productions of single beings before keyboards, the Age of Social Networks uncovered those selves in action, recording and saving the (hitherto hidden) ways in which the individual was transformed by others. The "I" became an active, instrumental verb that "One" could be even more justified now of circling. This new, interconnected social "I" at work, producing octopus-like protuberances that connected with the octoprotuberances of others, was an "I" even falser than the good old hubristic "I." The chief purpose of the new "I" of the social network was to lie; to pass on, that is, the social conventions that made it possible to be accepted. A non-conforming "self" could simply

[108] I'm limiting this insight strictly to the creative writer's archive. It is possible that data-mining not performed by robots can be useful to students of exact sciences who know what they are looking for, and know the digital world well enough to wander it like a terra incognita on the indeterminacy of a hunch, to find a proof or a new idea.

not exist in a social network, because there was nothing there to not conform to. Everything a social "I" transmits over the network is a plea for agreement with another octoprotuberance. The Social Network Age, which began with the classical purposes of virtuality to Survey and to Sell, eliminated the bureaucracies of surveillance and advertising by displaying, policing and selling all the information its members could articulate. What's more, the satisfaction level is high: the desires of the virtual "I"s of the social networks are for virtual objects that its members can make, sell and trade. The social networks have no need of the material world, though peoples' bodies are still a problem.

On the other hand, and this is the prestidigitator's other hand, if there is no present, past or future, the digital archive, in both its functions of inert storage and social interactivity, offers a huge opportunity for *play*. "I" can enter it at any point and at any time, "I" can and is "another(s)," and this I(s) can turn signs around, reverse chronologies, insert invented facts and ask "friends" to introduce their own fantasies into the archive. "I" can create its own scholars, biographers and heirs out of zeros and ones with a click of the typing digit.[109] I had once made print-people, with biographies, who saw the light through a complex combination of subterfuge, fake bios and careful contexts—a lot of bother in the distant age of print—so what was to stop me now, in the full digital bloom of millions of fantasy-creatures, from raiding my meager facts to make new archives that were like new people (complete with virtual sweat, tears, sperm, etc)? The works of these new people, who are all poets, can extend barely sketched notes to full potential; they can introduce any emotional context

[109] I type with only one finger: the *j'accuse* horizontally, God vertically and down keyboardingly; also known as "the trigger finger" (of my right hand).

with background music. I can collage, invent, collabo-
rate and ultimately reinvent the very self that the paper
Archives archives, and replace it with one that suits me
better. Yes, but only virtually. The paper Archives is still
*the material truth* (no matter how much it lies). Still,
to be able to play by giving birth to digital creatures is
like being a child again. Children have no trouble being someone else in a game, so why not assume roles
in the archive game in the same way? To the pleasure
of using the digital archive as a creative workshop instead of a repository, there is also the wicked delight of
altering the archives of others, which is what the Web
Bandit does. It would seem that thanks to the digital
Archives we have now come full circle to fulfilling the
dada-born utopian project of art's raison d'être: trans-
forming one's unique self and the selves of others into
a story with many happy endings that had been inconceivable in the pre-digital age. My physical "self" is
thus reduced to the fingerprint left by my typing finger
on the letters of my keyboard. Or, as is the case in many
computer games now, gestures (dance grimaces, winks)
can direct any number of avatars in any direction inside the social network. (All of it being, of course, a big
Inside.) Utopia (another one!) rises inevitably out of
the flattened digital landscape. Full digital commitment
makes the archive the only dwelling place of the posthuman, a creature that is an artist by default. The mass
migration of energetic posthumans into cyberutopia
is a fait-accompli. Everyone can tell a story in images,
dance, song, or words on a screen, and everyone does.
The social networks and games are a noisy city of artist
cafes and orgies that are a trillion gigabytes fuller and
louder than Baudelaire's Paris. Frequenters and participants are all users and abusers of their own and others'

archives; it's an artistic activity that can be as simple as gossip and as complex as a war (minus blood). For an artist (millions of us) virtuality offers no resistance: the digital archives is in constant use. Therefore, the digital archive can be trusted to provide the illusion of a coherent narrative (if it wants to) or a joyous chaos whose coherence is intrinsic but invisible. The only remaining difficulties are at the intersections of the posthuman digital world with what remains of humans. One of these is in the interface between the paper Archives and the digital archive: the flaws, the failures, the typos, the sweat, the traces of the human on the material, tell a dystopian story.[110] The human traces are not just at odds with the digital utopia, they are actively fighting it. The traces don't make (good) sense, even after they have been carefully catalogued, chronicled, preserved. What *happened* is mostly without happy endings. The road to the utopia of virtuality is not straight. There are piles of bodies. They stink. There is the threat of something called "nature." Virtuality in the paper library is no longer a competitor for stories with reality, but the repetitious mechanical producer of the same story in different formats. These intersections[111], where the digital utopians run into the human dystopians are battlegrounds. Only humans get hurt, because avatars feel no pain, but it is the pain itself that gives the human dystopia its power. The body, it turns out, is more complex than the bodies it generates in the virtual world. There are traces in the physical Archives that digitization

---

[110] Vide J.J. Phillips, previous footnote.

[111] These are not very grand, certainly not monumental, intersections: they are less impressive then the 1% genetic makeup that we don't share with chimpanzees; they measure only 0.1%.

cannot flatten. Just as there are traces of "something else" in poetry, just as there are exceptions, leftovers, mysteries, messes. Where do these things come from?

I'm getting ahead of myself here, so you can see what pull the future exercises already. Our present still has the one use that needs the human dirt: data-mining. In the factories of "social networks," which look like the idealized kibbutzim of yesteryear, we are voluntary workers. The owners of these factories mine us for advertising. They keep us under constant surveillance mainly for their profit, but they perform double-duty by providing the State with data for policing. In the glass house of the internet there are no secrets. However, as a poet I must cling to this transparency: through surveillance we still get an allowance for mystery and we can go on hoping for an ideal nondigital lover, maybe an olfactory critic, who will spring unexpectedly out of the make-believe and come lie down with us. It's a waning hope, designed to disappear when the police detect it. The National Security Agency looks for the signature of anyone who subverts the machine surveilling herm and terminates the subversive desire. There is an unresolved conflict between the interests of the Security State and the needs of advertisers: the State needs passive subjects, but advertisers need active desires. While this conflict goes on, we can take the opportunity to imagine that both the State and the advertisers who mine us find us intriguing enough to attend us. We live now in an Internetic Police State that can feel quite pleasant, very unlike the clunky old one I was born in. In the Romanian Police State, the microphones in the lightbulbs and the constant pressure to believe in the bright future of a 1925 sci-fi Soviet novel prevented unselfconscious communication with our social network (nonvirtual and small in those days). The Internet State is a Police State that uses a stylish pleasure-inducing device to take stock of our digits, instead of a thumb-screw. No one in their right mind would feel any nostalgia for the old way of obtaining fingerprints. The true distress is still a brief time off in the future when, having resolved their differences, the Security State and the advertisers will reach a detente by stimulating only harmless desires. When that happens we will miss the current Internet Police State because it still involved humans. In the coming Digital State the machine will police itself. Right now poetry still performs its rites because the human-controlled digital police still patrol ideas as if they were things. Wishing to be physically archived now means wishing for this not-entirely Digital State, attentive for whatever reason. Enjoy it, it won't last long. When the human police go away, this modicum of attention will collapse, leaving us talking in the e-void. We do miss the police, do we not? as Cavafy might have said, but didn't (it would be way too utopian to dream of "barbarians" now; the most one can hope for is a bored policeman in *front* of a screen; when the shift changes, the new policeman will be *inside* the screen, just like you and me). Even advertising is at this time an affirmation of our physical humanity. Being mined for obscure yearnings and turning these into a desire to acquire something is still a validation of the body. Not exactly poetry, but it is a kind of reading, a concession pure data makes for human contradictions. The detente between virtual surveillance and advertising will eventually empty us of our contradictions[112], but the resulting utopia will still be kinder than the one I was born in. For one thing, it won't hurt the flesh, which used

[112] When they have broken them into all the component parts that might conceivably want something.

to hurt terribly. The new State will disappear the flesh slowly, bit by bit, and painlessly. All police states are flesh-eaters, and what fuels them is *optimism*. In the country I grew up in, optimism was compulsory; in the world that places its human weaknesses in the hope of virtual perfection, optimism is unconscious and ubiquitous, like air. But make no mistake: the goal is the same, namely "the new man."

One condition that neither the real nor the virtual world can remedy is *loss*. The job of humans fighting machines now is to lose optimism, the fuel that powers the police. My lost notebook, for instance, *must* stay lost: finding it now would only restore the police state it was lost in. The true enemy of the state (and our hero) is not the teenage poet who lost it, but the thief who stole it, even if "the thief" was just negligence. Only thieves stand between the old utopian police state of my adolescence and the digital police state of my posthumanity, and these precious thieves must be fiercely defended. The digital state is already hunting them by programming "clean machines" to patrol the cracks we most prize (because that's where we lose stuff). Poetry will still be the default religion of the human remnant if it protects thieves from "clean machines" now. In other words, our poems must be hiding places for thieves, or they'll become blueprints for archival machines. I must now speak a machine language to hide a poem. (*Long space filled with gibberish here.*)

The physical Archives inhabits a world that exists in parallel (but only physically) with an unarchived repository, the Unarchive, the Negative Archive.[113] This Unarchive contains all that is omitted, deliberately or

[113] This is different from the "Dispersed Archives," which, tenuously, but still, has a material presence.

unknowingly, from the Archives. There is no doubt that such an Unarchive exists, and that it is in fact richer, deeper and larger than any current Archive. Every document recorded, or realized and stored, is accompanied by an undocumented, unrecorded, unrealized version that was aborted at some point. It is unimportant what prevents a document from being saved: the withholding is a refusal of the existential imprimatur.[114] The Unarchive is filled by potentialities, by facts that are de facto flaws, magnified flaws, flaws magnified so greatly they didn't acquire a retainable shape. The world of these shadows, aborted forms, whirls like a dust storm around and between the cracks in our Archives. Still, they exist in potential form: the poem that could have been written instead of the one that was; the novel that didn't novelize; the essay that tried but couldn't. These unrealized forms, enemies of the archived product, are the shadow army that defends an unfathomable Unarchive. The existence of the Unarchive is unquestionable because: a) the Archive has gaps[115], and b) discovery (in all human areas) is predicated by a *missing something* in the official record. The rhetoric of "overthrowing," as in "Einstein overthrew Newton" is wrong: Einstein didn't "overthrow" Newton, Einstein found the gap, the missing element in Newton's physics. Science, like poetry, evolves through the investigation of gaps, of

---

[114] I say "existential" rather than "political" because the existence of a record is a larger reality than the evident political manipulation of most "history." The "existence" of the record is the work of many shadow entities, only some of which are "political"; others may be biological or mineral.

[115] Evident to painting restorers, for instance, who make a career of filling in what should have been there. It's mostly a guess though, so I'd get a second opinion every time.

the missing elements, of *exceptions*. The Archive is the repository of rules, the Unarchive contains the exceptions. The problem is not whether the Unarchive exists or not, but whether the Unarchive is amenable to digital reinvention. If digitized, it certainly is, but only in digital form. In its nondigital form it eludes the utopian grasp of the digital. Sensibilities in search of gaps in the physical Archives[116] often find in them the same creative impulses that drive digital posthumans to create utopias, but unlike the digital utopians, they cannot reconcile the a priori[117] dystopian narratives with the actual archival objects. The competent researcher

---

[116] If my Unarchive had produced its objects (or *has*, as per revised rejectionist language-defense), it would have still had the same intention as my present archive: to sabotage the narratives of Archives in ways that would allow the Archives of Amnesia to pour through into the present. This sabotage consists in making holes, making the flawless holey. The December 1989 Romanian flag with the hole in it where the communist anthem was cut out was one such successfully pierced narrative. The archeology of amnesia probes the sanctioned stories until it finds a weak spot to poke a hole into, enter it (the way I returned from my quarter of a century exile back to Romania) and, once inside, recreate from suppressed artifacts an erased history. The recreated artifact may be only a newer story, another word-object, but it has (for a time) a brighter existence, the brighter the longer it spent underground. The archeology of amnesia must work very fast to make its holes because official narrative is made of quickly regenerative tissue. Holes close quicker and quicker now (the Romanian hole in the flag was patched within two weeks of the success of the Revolution). Sometimes the "revolution" is between quotes, the truth—which I suspect of being at least half-true—would put the "hole" in the flag in quotes too, a much graver matter; a "hole" between quotes is pure disinformation, naked propaganda. A political essay on the Archeology of Amnesia by Steven Duplantier and Max Cafard in *Neotropica 3* (2010), lists chronologically the disastrous forays of the United States in Central America, a list all but erased by most recent histories of the region. I once had the privilege of being given a marvelous tour of Chicago's "uncommemorated history" by Thomas Frank, a historian of the American labor movement: He took me to an empty lot in an abandoned area in Chicago's South Side where Republic Steel Pinkertons killed hundreds of striking workers in the early 20th century; we visited the site of the Haymarket Riots, and I heard the remarkable story of its various monuments and their destruction over the years; we visited the graves of anarchists, the little-tended grave of Emma Goldman, and many more historical sites overgrown by weeds and neglect. Doubtlessly, an archeology and geography of Amnesia can be a profitable business for any historian or aficionado of the Deliberately Forgotten. The presence of reminders is mostly composed of the exclamation points of winners, as outside scholars point out, but it's also made of places signed by an orthography of uncertainty, bad record-keeping and literal forgetting. One should be weary of flawless archival narratives: there aren't any except the world itself.

[117] An addendum to Foucault's "historical a priori" in *The Archeology of Knowledge*.

looks for "negative space," the "negative poetic" of John Keats. The Unarchive is not a metaphysics, it is what makes possible the past, and that past's archive. The physical Unarchive and the physical Archives are amenable only to interpretation, commentary and e-consideration: they are not movable through time. Even the flat e-archive derived from the physical Archives has to reveal (through time discontinuities, contradictions, paradoxes, incompatibilities, etc.) *where* the gaps are. A researcher who goes there must begin to work in the negative poetics of the missing to uncover first a history, then a potential reality, then a virtual world, and then, maybe, a reason to continue, to make room for an *heir*. The flat e-archive makes the discovery more difficult[118], maybe even impossible, since the utopian digital impulse will do its best to blind the researchers to these gaps. The Unarchive is more fluid, more tenuous, and more elusive than the Archive, because its unrealized projects faded inside the brains that failed to realize them or, even worse, these DOA projects have sometimes taken on archival masks, like zombies pretending to be alive.[119] The digital archive

[118] As well as demanding from the researcher great faith in the impossibility of perfection. The degree of skepticism required of a guerillero researcher ready to take on the perfection of the digital is awesome, like that of Diogenes.

[119] J.J. Phillips' comments on the Unarchives in this essay follow her visceral account of the Brautigan material:

*For reasons not entirely clear to me, TBL (Bancroft Library) is driven to insure that the literally corporeal element (desiccated brain matter and cerebral fluid on the page) be part of the Unarchives, even as they are physically part of his archive and available to be examined; yet to me, these pages constitute THE most important and profound aspect of Brautigan's archives. The need of TBL to treat it as part of his Unarchives, and even deceive people about what it IS, has been troubling to me for a variety of reasons, and I realize now that I needed your term/dimension "Unarchives" to be able to probe this question. They are textual fetishists but why is this artifact taboo, when it should be enshrined with pride of place as a holy literary relic. The horrors! The horrors! Where the word made flesh is entombed – to think of 'passion' in both the ordinary and the Aristotelian senses, more or less. Also there are the scatological qualities of an impacted bowel – all très freudian. However, I fear this desire will remain part of my Unarchive, in the private charnel house of my desires, since I'll probably never write it. Was never a fan of Brautigan's writing, his genius escapes me, but I am rather perversely fascinated by his life, and then his death. Brautigan's act, incredibly sad and horrific as it was, makes a profound and indelible statement about a whole lot of things; however, at the same time my mind is drawn to such cogitations, it rebels at having to think about the violent disintegration of somebody else's brain, whether I like his writing or not.*

J.J. has other fascinating comments on the physical aspect of archive/unarchives, but the secret she reveals here is shocking: this particular Archives (but, most likely, all Archives) *hide* the morbid facts of their occupation, and thus deprive researchers of what is most vital to viewing an original document: the Human Stain. The implication here is that the Unarchive is the night of the Archive's day. The overt purpose of an Archives is to shed light on the past, which is impossible without hiding the darkness of the past. The digital is palliative, no matter how well it copies the original, even including its morbid grain. It's a safe bet, however, that the morbid traces will never be digitized until an underground community of hacker-archivists makes it its business to reproduce gore, flaws and errors—and *only* gore, flaws and errors. There is no substitute for horror. Horror is the inadmissible truth of history, any history, and is only available to the researcher in the original trace. One might label a virtual exposition of Holocaust objects "horror," but nothing will approximate the loneliness of a scholar touching a pair of reading glasses found at Auschwitz, except the Unarchive of the is helpless when faced with zombies. Some unrealized projects exist in the memories of witnesses where they might be twisted like branches by the winds of the official record: compromised memory, manipulated recordings, false memories, worn recitations. To know what's missing and what is distorted is a tall order, a small task perhaps to future minds moving inside Archives as easily as we move through a parking lot[120], but going against the utopian urge of the digital will prove insurmountable.

So I surrendered my private archive to the future's bright cherry-pickers, but the Unarchive remained untouched. Therein lay issues not covered by a facile reading of archival libraries as institutional servants of power. Yes, archives are used by ideologues in or out of power to tell one or another story. Yes, there are archivists who think themselves the Johnny Appleseed(s)[121] of knowledge, who see the mission of the digital to

(flesh) person who once wore them. The curator of such objects will be driven to madness; archivists are both mad and required by the job to hide their madness; they are civilization's most accomplished liars and fetishism is but a small consolation. One might well wonder how I could compare the curator/archivist of a Holocaust museum/library with the keeper of, let's say, a collection of history-of-science books and manuscripts, but this is precisely where J.J.'s experience erases the distinction. There are degrees of Horror, of course, but they reside only in their sensual provenance, in the original. One can imagine and empathize with the copy, but that empathy is palliative. What one feels about a copy is a copy of a feeling.

[120] These would be the skeptic(s) mentioned above.

[121] "'As an archivist you kind of think like Johnny Appleseed,'" David Fleming on the subject of digitizing the vast Alan Lomax Folk Center recordings and documents. ("Folklorist's Global Jukebox Goes Digital" by Larry Rohter, *The New York Times*, January 30, 2012) There is a good argument to be made that the easy availability of a visionary collection like the one assembled by Alan Lomax would make an "accidental" encounter more likely. The "digital vagabonds" making use of random objects are already at work among us, but I'll stand firm on the idea that even the most brilliant discovery is still a "mirroring," not a physical "other." Robert Creeley's line, "the body is the plan" will never be displaced by "the plan is *something like* the body." Ishi, last of the humans, takes a bow. But then he dies (archived, in the museum).

make knowledge ubiquitously available. The first view is dystopian, the second utopian, but neither covers the random encounter of a researcher with the material in "the neighborhood." The digital "neighborhood," even recreated to scale, is not a physical archive any more than a digital bookstore is a bookstore. Future minds may wonder in digital space the way bodies move now in physical space, but what will they discover? Mirrors. There is more now in the inert innards of a physical Archives than the self-interest of researchers; there are, for instance, objects without any use until found by accident.[122] The truly new, the unexpected, is rarely uncovered by a self-interested search, it is *always* the fruit of an accident, the revelation of a gap[123] in the physical store. The "other" is not digital, whatever the arrow-sharp "self" in search of a specific thing is. "I" may be digital but "you" are not. No randomized search will ever create a miraculous "other" because a miracle is by definition outside algorithms, as any gambler can

[122] The Reader has surely noted by now that writing on "archive" can be done only in a most specific and narrow sense, hopefully the most specific and narrowest sense. This essay began as an effort to render concisely my relationship with Archives and archivists, as concerns my personal papers and library. The richness of the subject thwarted that intention immediately, but I have resisted as much as I can the tendency of the word "archive" and all its echoes, ramifications, and seductions, to take on everything in the world. A quick survey of philosophical or specialized writings on "archive" sees that every writer on the subject was faced by this problem: a subtitle indicating the borders of the discussion is almost always called for. Jacques Derrida's essay *Archive Fever* is subtitled a "psychoanalytical view," and takes the form of a rewritten speech delivered by Derrida at the Freud museum in London, and keeps the reins tightly on an archival reflection about the transformation of Freud's "home" into a "museum." Even this focus broadens despite itself like a river overrunning its banks, because the distinction between Freud's "home," which was the repository of the bourgeois psyche of the German-speaking European fin-de-siècle, was already a huge "archive," and its transformation into a "museum" is the only possibility the essay has to narrow the philosophical immensity by introducing the public (curated) dimensions of the repository. My essay might be subtitled redundantly "an archival memoir," which is redundant only until a distinction is made between my frail human memory and the larger (though still holey) archive reposing in Baton Rouge and Urbana-Champaign. My memory has this advantage over the stored documents, however: it can remember things that cannot be confirmed by the record, and it can invent things that are. A writer's work exists on at least three contiguous planes: persona memory, archive documents, and "finished" works that have been distributed, but do not belong to either their author or to the archive: they are the readers.

[123] Or the intrusion of the Unarchive into the well-ordered objects before the bored researcher on the long library table. There is some cosmology here, an appeal to string theory perhaps, but we'd be foolish to surrender any here-and-now to a theory.

tell you. "Luck" is always physical. The neurologist will see you now. But not very well. He's blind. Meet Mr. Borges.

David Faulds' accidental discovery of the Renata Pescanti Botti's book-notebook is one such object that turned out for me to be the mouth of a tunnel leading to interesting places. The presence of this Unarchive-pointing object proves the uniqueness of the physical Archives, which *cannot be erased*. No matter how much digital imagination and skill a posthuman might use to recreate the past, herm could not possibly create this object. The Botti book-notebook can only be physically born. It is impossible to destroy this subject by distorting, collaging or altering any digital copy. You can erase its scan from a drive or a Cloud; it could have a myriad lives within infinitely multiplying drives and clouds, it could shrink, grow, change, disappear or be reprinted, but the original could not be digitally altered because it was not digital-born. A physical-born object can only exist digitally as a *copy*.

Even if one follows the labyrinth that is the "self" through the genetic blueprint, one cannot predict or create digitally what the flesh of that "self" made. Physical origin can only be reproduced physically. Virtuality can reproduce but it cannot *create*.

There is an anecdote, apocryphal perhaps, that the library that acquired for a pretty penny the papers of poet Robert Creeley, refused to pay anything for a large email correspondence between Creeley and Norman Mailer. The story makes sense, even if it was just a brief fin-de-siècle panic among my confreres. Why should a

building preserve what are infinitely reproducible electronic messages? In these letters there are no smudges,
no odd pauses of the keys, no whiff of tobacco or per-
fume, no ink blots, no erasures. The *pain* and *pleasure*
of the writer are invisible. And that is what in effect a
good old-fashioned archive preserves: pain, flaws, whiffs
of bygone bodies, the evidence of the unseen surround
flowing through the writer's finger(s) unto the paper.
That's where the openings leading to the Unarchive
are. The perfect, infinitely reproducible electronic
copy erases these flawed and spontaneous openings,
that is to say, the human handiwork. In the eArchive
humans exist without bodies: there are no hands, no
sweat, no tears, no blood, no fluids of any kind. These
were eliminated by the word-processors which left only
the *meaning*. The authors of these perfect, meaning-
ful e-texts are schematic beings without bodies; they
are biographies-reduced-to-cerebral-intentions. My
archive at Hill may be among the last living authors'
paper archives, but one day it will be digitized and then
only a diligent being shaped by secret vestigial senses
will correctly (mis)understand me. Hopefully, partisan
archivists (who will, by then, be a resistance army, a
guerilla force) will build my golem-totem from zeros
and ones, just as easily as they would from physical evidence. Thanks, guerilla people! Viva the Gap!™ But
first, you must undo the utopian urge of the digital, a
tall order that goes against the posthuman digital Prime
Imperative: the Happy Ending.

I didn't always appreciate archivists as guerillas, until
I saw them as future myselves. Before the advent of
the internet, the archival enterprise was a conundrum.
I fancied myself an anarchist and a utopian. Can either

anarchism or utopia have a physical archive? There are archives of the history of both, but can the act of anarchist destruction or heavenward inspiration be archived? This is a question I couldn't ask before losing my virginities, my first public, hence archival, acts. Before then I existed in a potential, weightless state, with some faith in language, but no traces of it worth keeping. The adolescent's lost notebook put starkly the question of the archive: I had the choice to be free and weightless in a miserable world, or extrude a shell of significance to carry on my back until it became too heavy and had to be deposited in good samaritan buildings. This choice confronts every adolescent. Emily Dickinson knew how dreadful it was to be "somebody," but chose it despite her claim that the "somebody" in her poem was not her. It was her and only her, a "somebody" who acquired an archive as soon as she publicly dissed herself. Dickinson might have gotten away with it if she'd never come out, but come out she did, modestly, but irremediably. As for me, I have too much archivism in myself: being a Jew I am archival from birth, or at least from my bris[124]; my whole grab-bag of identities is the portable sack of a hobo bandit. What I carry in there are weapons I called "identities" because I didn't want to put my contemporaries on the defense. I wanted them to love me, even if I was out to fight them. In my twenties, my literary efforts were partly designed to confuse the archive: I made up people who didn't exist, wrote letters in places that pretended to be other places, committed archive-scrambling pranks whenever possible. My generational colleagues did the same. Keith Abbott's magazine, *Blue Suede Shoes*, published fractional issues: he imagined the Dewey decimal system screaming (his name). We did these things from

[124] "Inscribed from birth by a loss, archived as a 'lack,' meaning 'chosen.'" -Jacques Derrida, *Archival Fever* (translated by Eric Prenowitz; The University of Chicago Press, 1995).

an instinctive distrust of order, symbolized for us by libraries. Power depended on orderly systems in every area of life, and we tried to subvert it in our practice. Ideally, this should be a delightful era for archivists to look back on, because our tricks were transparent and fun. Theoretically, they will provide the basis for another system. You won't have Dewey to knock around much longer, as Nixon said. The digitization of all writing changes everything, including our Sixties naive sense of fun: it is an event bigger than Nixon (who was not the last powerful man who tried to cover up his crimes while recording them[125]). Digitization makes everything transparent, thus making both hiding and morality obsolete.

To this, Elaine Smyth noted, "But what if, in fact, digitization makes everything opaque? After all you can't see the digital object unmediated with the naked eye— you must have the machine, and it must be the right machine and it must have the right software on it. (Am I just insisting I will never be posthuman?) Otherwise you are very definitely stuck with the dystopian version: the download will only ever be surfing the general statistical wave, you'll never have certain access to any individual/individual object." There is a time-stamped agreement here: in 2012 we do know more about preserving cellulose than pixels; the flatness of the pixel document may very well be opaque, its transparency virtual; virtual transparency makes the sleight-of-hand (the machine-reader) unnoticeable to the human reader whose machine-reader functions. The trick is revealed only by a malfunctioning machine-reader, a technical

[125] Tape-recording (analog) is the immediate precursor of the digital.

problem that may be solved by the time this is published, it is solved as we speak. The architectures' only
job is to make themselves small and invisible while digitizing the world and creating virtual copies of it. Micro-
processors' function is to store and manipulate memory
on a smaller and smaller scale; their architecture is light
as spores, but its illusions can be any scale your printer
chooses, making it possible to create a physical object
from the past.  Elaine offered a link, http://blogs.loc.
gov/digitalpreservation/2011/12/the-artifactual-
elements-of-born-digital-records-part-2/ (itself full of
links), to a post called *The Artifactual Elements of Born-
Again Digital Records, Part 2* (posted on December
5th, 2011 by Bill LeFurgy):

> *A previous post suggested how the digital
> environment within computer programs and sys-
> tems creates an artifactual element to born-digital
> records. An analog equivalent to this idea can be
> found in the popular Thomas Jefferson's Library ex-
> hibit here at the Library of Congress. This re-creation
> of Jefferson's library maintains Jefferson's original
> cataloging system and also recreates the unique cir-
> cular construction of his bookcases. Clearly, how Jef-
> ferson arranged his books and shelves adds meaning
> to the collection. The artifactuality of his library
> itself, not just its content, influences our interpreta-
> tion and understanding of him as a historic figure.
> The Thomas Jefferson of today, however, would be-
> queath some zip disks or an old laptop to be preserved;
> and instead of recreating library shelving, digital
> archivists will be recreating operating systems or
> software programs. The process of recreating an ob-
> solescent program or digital environment within a*

*contemporary computer system is generally known as emulation. A popular way to recreate video games from outmoded consoles, emulation is also being used in libraries and archives as a way to preserve the artifactual characteristics of born-digital archival collections. One such emulation project is Emory University Manuscript, Archives, and Rare Book Library's recreation of Salman Rushdie's computer. Through emulation, a researcher can use a workstation in MARBL's reading room that recreates the exact "native digital environment" of Rushdie's now-obsolete computer. The emulation provides access to Rushdie's original programs, directories, and files just as he experienced them. The emulation program even opens in a window the exact same size as Rushdie's original computer screen. A video explaining this can be seen here.[126]*

Please note that, once again, (M)Emory is involved, and that a new concept is launched: "artifactuality." The digital has now leapt ahead of the "real" by creating virtual environments that "emulate" both software and born-digital documents and the space where they were first created (Salman Rushdie's writing desk and

[126] The explanation continues:

*Other repositories are exploring similar emulation projects. Sanford has tested emulating the original word-processing program upon which some born-digital collections were created. Similarly, Maryland Institute for Technology in the Humanities, has investigated emulation as a means of access to its Deena Larson Marble Springs Collection. On a broader scale, the EU KEEP project and the UK PLANETS project have both worked to provide access to a variety of digital objects through emulation services. As well, the PARADIGM project, the British LibraryDigital Lives Project, the AIMS project, and NEH/IMLS-funded RESEARCH have all explored issues in supporting born-digital personal collections across a variety of archival activities including using emulation as a preservation and access strategy. Beyond personal digital collections, the NDIIPP-sponsored Preserving Virtual Worlds investigated ways to preserve video games, interactive content, and complete online*

*environments. As cultural heritage institutions access an increasing amount of born-digital material and as format and hardware obsolescence accelerates, preserving the artifactual elements of born-digital material will remain a challenge. While emulation provides one means of supporting access and preservation, emulating every obsolescent system or program is no more realistic than preserving every document. Just as born-digital records have forced the digital preservation community to develop new methods for ensuring authenticity, they will also require new understandings of how to preserve information, artifactuality, and context.*

I have erased every link in the preceding paragraph because I'm not a travel agency for the jargon-challenged. But note that what is being said is: only us (the links) can recreate a significant environment because the only significant environment is one that has the money (Disney). I would no more trust Disney to create my "reality" than the writer of the above apology, who is a mouthpiece for the Disney equivalent of archiving.

computer). The computer on Rushdie's desk is not a prop: it is his computer. The user of the Rushdie v-room isn't just a visitor, a spectator, or a note-taker: herm can enter it, see his e-desktop and everything in it, and then sit down and finish the unfinished writing in there using the keyboard. All writers of the digital age are now subject to new writers of the digital age who can enter their computers to finish, change, revise or rewrite the "original" work. Any digital-born writing thus becomes a collaboration. It can only be called "original" between quotes, because no matter who initiated it, this writing is still subject only to collaboration and copying; its physical origin remains unique. "Original" still means "the first," and it is subject only to virtual *revision*, that is to say reproduction. The architecture of the space where the digital file waits to be "raised" (after being "born") will be no more than just a video-game, no matter how "realistic." The space (the architectural and the written) can be re-translated to factual materiality by the depth of any visitor's desire. You want to just *look*? Fine. You want to *participate*? OK, as little or as much as you desire. But you will only be seeing copies, simulations. The visitor can translate hermself to any desired virtuality and back. A writer who wants to finish an unfinished Rushdie story can reach out and, absent-mindedly, stroke Rushdie's crystal ball or, why not, his cat: but only via the simulation. It might even be possible, in the not far future, to "factualize" or materialize the cat via a 3-D printer, but the original cat will keep purring in the *live* past it inhabits without even noticing its virtual existence. In Rushdie's particular case, the inspiration for *Midnight's Children* came from the *1001 Nights*, a collection of tales that abound in mechanical-human hybrids[127] that

[127] *The automaton, a creature who is neither living nor dead, features frequently in the Nights . . . The brass oarsman who bears a tablet of lead inscribed with talismanic characters on his breast and who rows the Third Dervish to the Island of Safety; the little manikin which a dervish fashions out of beeswax and which plunges into the river to retrieve the sultan's lost signet ring; the air-driven statues which seem to speak . . . and the Ebony Horse, which is powered by wind and, when the right lever is pulled, carries a man through the air: they all simulate life, but there is no life in them.* - Robert Irwin, *The Arabian Nights: A Companion*

are prototypes for the digital-born. But they have no life: they are mechanical. They can acquire lookalikes, digital kin that may even contain spliced human genes, but they are lifeless. Gene-spliced digital-born creatures may resemble life very closely, but they are not real. Simulations are aleatory and illusory.[128] What can be imagined can be digitally joined to what it describes and even to what it suggests, but never to what it *is*. The fictional setting of a novel can be digitally recreated to be nonfictional, for instance, but the conscious and unconscious life the embodied writer charged herm sentences with cannot be reproduced. No matter the form, the hand has left the trace of its origin in the manuscript. This trace is no longer visible in the older virtuality of the printed book, but it's even less visible in the perfected(ed) image of the digital copy. A writer's imaginary environment can be digitally recreated, the computer can even search the psychological range from which sprang the writer's choice of phrasing, and create the work's exegesis, but in the end it will still be only a perfected virtuality. I have no doubt that virtual technology can produce the writer, complete with herm critics, but without *the body*. The digital-born can reproduce the development and the hermeneutics of an imaginary object, beginning at any point; it can begin with the *suggested* and end with a *history*; it can produce the socius, the architecture and the cloned writer starting in any of these—and it can then translate (print) all

[128] I can hear the great cry of protest arising now: "Clones are alive!" cry the partisans of clones, cloned themselves (perhaps) eons ago. You'll just have to take this on faith: the science will come later. Clones may be very much like the original, but they are not the original. The missing ingredient, invisible to the hopeful eye, is the "life," an assembly of neural connections collected by the senses from a particular zeitgeist. This life assembly, a sort of constantly balancing gyroscope, is the soul. *The soul is the body at work in its own time.* Not clonable. There is no contradiction here between my earlier "everything is alive" act of the creative imagination, and this affirmation of "the soul." What is the distinction exactly between a seemingly inert (inorganic, in old parlance) object with soul, and a soulless object, is to be found in the quality of the creation itself. The virtual is soulless, especially if identical with the soulful. The copy just don't cut it.

of it into the physical world, but it still cannot produce its origin in the nondigital past. An Archives can be a playpen, a rookery, a store of endless virtualities (including books) but its gravity will remain concentrated in the Human Stain.

The Human Stain is the *un*imaginable, the kind of game with personae and facts that poets play in order to question "truth." Authenticity will always remain a problem for the digital, just as it is for the real. What's more, a subversive flesh-based poetics sees to it that there is no "hard" guarantee that the content offered by the machine-reader is the same as the input. This is because the digital can only be *true* insofar as it is *born*, just like any other product of birth, whether flesh or paper. The digital-born, like the woman-born or the mind-born, must first exist in order to be falsified, diverted, thwarted or disappeared. The *first* output can never be a forgery, it must exist before it can be forged. After it's been forged it can become a forgery of a forgery ad infinitum, maybe even an exact negative of the input, a mirror image. When the digital seems to transcend (as in Andrea's tats being "read" by a scanner, for ex) the emulation (mimetic) stage, it only *seems* to erase origin; a digital first is a skeuomorph that mimics origin(ality). Digital-born virtualities will give reality a run for the money, but only when the Archives of Amnesia are full. The digital will be able to *print* reality, making it seemingly impossible to tell which came first.[129] The energy needed to translate back into materials like flesh or paper the creations of the digital-born will exhaust all material resources, including anything "hard" about the reading/imaging machines themselves (which will have moved, for convenience, inside

[129] This has already happened many times. Plato's "ideal" was the digital.

us). This may begin (as it already has) a retro-artistic motion that will quickly become humanity's *only* occupation (after forgetting the body in the Archives of Amnesia's innermost chamber). This fascinating race between the real and the virtual, whose starter pistol has already gone off, will be stumbling only over the question of memory. How "real" is the real, how "virtual" is the virtual, how "real" *was* the "virtual," and how virtual *was* the "real"? In other words, did the originator of the object make a "true" object, or something quite different, as per a diversionary art-originated object that may seem (or even be) identical, but exists in a parallel world.

But what if the digital object was created for the purpose of distorting or disappearing its physical truth?[130] Why would anyone do such a thing? Certainly not G-d? Hippies? Performance artists? The Devil's Jokers? Or just a writer covering herm tracks with writing? Writing itself is a mask, a diversionary virtual object meant to hide whatever was there in the first place. Every inscribed surface is a palimpsest, a labyrinth for hiding the writer, but why? Let's backtrack a bit, then jet forth again to the Library of Congress (the grand rookery of the digital-born) again. Toward the end of the 20th century, when the digital took hold, bureaucracies did not completely trust pixels: employees made paper copies of every e-mail in case they needed a "paper trail." This archival (or defensive) effort printed out digital-born documents; the back-and-forth between digitization and print provided a political safeguard, but it obligated the Archives to store both the digital-born

---

[130] A visit to the origin room at the Archives of Amnesia can clear it all up.

and the print copy. Briefly, the storage space looked like it was growing instead of shrinking. The angst of the archivist, preserver, restorer and researcher was that the digital mutated so fast that its languages quickly became obsolete and illegible, along with the hardware needed to translate them. Eventually, an Archives would have to store the history of history along with the means of (re)producing it, becoming in the process a palimpsest of writing and writing technologies, a palimpsest that may have been created for the purpose of covering *something up*. Simultaneously, the ease with which anyone could produce internet-only material led all those professionals to fear that they (as well as everyone else) would soon mistake the digital-born for nature and *believe* in its immanent permanence. This "belief" in nature is rationally suspect, but inevitable: speaking only of writing, everything that seems "natural" now underwent a process of abstraction that absorbed or replaced a "harder" reality—think clay tablets versus goatskin, goatskin versus paper: as the materials became more pliable, more "evanescent," their presence and influence increased, and so did our confidence, a confidence that need only become unconscious to be a "belief." We now literally write with "light," whereas we once used chemical dye. Digital information *will be* the new nature, there is no alternative, at least until another nature shows up. The digital-born Archives is nicely complete in the Rushdie example, a good vantage point from which to reflect back on the relationship between the real and the digital-born. William James makes for a good midpoint between Thomas Jefferson and Salman Rushdie. He writes that, "A favorite way of opposing the more abstract to the more concrete account is to accuse those who favor the latter of 'confounding psychology with logic.' Our critics say that when we are asked what truth MEANS, we reply by telling only how it is ARRIVED-AT. But since a meaning is a logical relation, static, independent of time, how can it possibly be identified, they say, with any concrete man's experience, perishing as it does at the instant of its production?" And, in another context, "The most ancient parts of truth also once were plastic. They also were called true for human reasons. They also mediated between still earlier truths and what in those days were novel observations. Purely objective truth, truth in whose establishment the function of giving human satisfaction in marrying previous parts of experience with newer parts played no role whatsoever, is nowhere to be found. The reasons why we call things true is the reason why they are true, for 'to be true' means only to perform this marriage-function."[131] Is there anything left untended when the environment of Thomas Jefferson, including his understanding of nature (which is his psychology) are digitally-reborn? Is there an empty space, a suture, a tiny cavity where the something like "the soul" might reside? There isn't, as first-year anatomy students discover in their first dissection. Both the real and the virtual are perfect, in that they leave no room for doubt as to their "truth." And still we put "truth" between quotes, because it is true now, but it also contains the full consciousness and mechanism for being fraudulent in fifteen minutes... which is when this body stands up to take a break and says "Nonsense!" The virtual doesn't have to pee. "He" remains seated. "He" never imagined this need, especially right now when things seem to be going so well for the virtual.

To the stages of my writing at different ages and for

[131] "Pragmatism's Conception of Truth" Lecture 6 in *Pragmatism: A New Name for Some Old Ways of Thinking*, William James (Longman Green and Co, 1907).

different purposes, you can now add the coverup legitimized by the Archives. But again, why? What emergency requires the intense effort of such vast journeys of translation between the real and the virtual and back? Why do we need the *un*imaginable? And why do we need time? I could return to St. Augustine here to make the grammatical argument of tenses as states of awareness, but why does one need language at all? Only language needs time, and it needs less and less of it, just like Archives need less and less room. All tenses, all senses, and all the storage of them fit inside an infinitesimal point. It is that point which began expanding and requiring time, space, language, self, and self-production and (re)production. And it is at the limit of that expending point that virtuality makes it possible to, again, dispense with all the above. This little philosophical incursion is itself just a jumping-off point to the *un*imaginable, the Unarchive. The infinitesimal point's expansion(s) all seem perfect, until that *un-* is introduced. What to do with pure negativity, Dada? Call it death-wish or poetics, call it virtual or mimetic, call it what you want, go with Hegel or go with Kant, put it on a slice or stick it in a bun, it all goes home to that *un-*.[132]

The world is the Archives of everything in it. Language is itself an Archives that orders the complexities of the world in order to communicate them. Writing is the Archives of the Archives of language: it orders the complexities of communicating the extant knowledge for the purpose of stabilizing them. Each Archives is the codification of a previous Archives, and each new Archives intends to simplify the communication of knowledge, an intention that acquires complexity as soon as

[132] This rap inspired by Jim Gustafson's *No Money in Art* (Alternative Press, cc.1982).

it is codified, requiring a new Archives. There is no telling how many Archives there are, but a writer's project can only be an Archives, which brings me back to my lined, lost notebook. Those lines signified the borders of my world. Going beyond them, into the unknown, into the religion of poetry, was a (necessary) delusion. Had I suspected that my writing was going to be a lifelong effort to end up in an institutional Archives, I'd have given it up, no matter what plauds I garnered. The truth, however, is that the Archives is the intrinsic reason for performing the act of writing, which is already an Archives by the time it leaves the hand. The hope of any writing is to create an Archives good enough to communicate the writer's adventures in the Archives of language. Genre differences are deceptive: a journalist might believe that herm is "reporting an event," but herm is only reporting the language that archives the event. Poetry alone, among the many kinds of writing, has the ability to not pretend that it is about anything other than the poet's adventures in the Archives of language. (I say that it has "the ability," because many poets, including myself, believe((d)) that poetry had the force to act directly on matter in demiurgic ways.) What "One" may have been circling was the loci of hubris. He intuited early what we now all know, namely that in the Age of the Archive, when everything can be known, the only language still living is poetry, or the memoir (in the sense of Frank O'Hara's *In Memory of My Feelings*). Poetry so invested has the great burden of shedding received ideas and available information, its instrumental "I" first of all. The "I" must get out of the way of the world, spake "One."

In a digitized world, where storage doesn't require a

lot of room, archival libraries will merge with museums. It's a dire prospect. If to this moment I granted the library Archives significance (to the point of giving it the company of an Unarchive), I now have to darken the image. The archive-museum merger threatens to destroy language; it will even dissolve the question "why language?" Truth or fiction, archival or unarchival, my concerns are mostly with language, preserved, destroyed, distorted, but language still. Every word, whether on deposit or not, is an archive; it has an etymology, a history, it travels through languages; it is understandable and imaginable. Language belongs everywhere. Everything humans know is deposited in the words they speak, so keeping a record of past words is a luxury, a redundancy, a market for architectural ideas, a store of vanities.[133] Museums are another matter; they are not about language; they are about artifacts and location. They are collections of artifacts that have been removed from the places where they were made. Nothing in a museum *belongs*: everything in it was taken, torn, bought from its birthplace.[134] The museum must consistently exhibit the

---

[133] The utopian version: the Archives is a backup of someone who thinks hermself worthy of a backup. In the future, a less cumbersome direct download of the entire person will be available to anyone. The dystopian version: the download has the gap (the *un-*) that will never allow the reconstitution of any person, but can serve as a story-line for statistical analysis.

[134] Elaine Smyth comments: "But isn't the same true of libraries – at least libraries up to the end of the 20th century? The physical artifacts of books are powerful beyond the language they embody, as several of the stories in your memoir (thus far) attest." Yes, but books are, with rare exceptions, multiples. Museum artifacts are, with exceptions, unique, having served a physical function in a cultural- or bio-complex.

original sin(s) of appropriating, naming, and ordering them.

It was still possible, for as long as it took you to read this book, to distinguish the quickly vanishing border[135] between the real and the virtual. This essay is a history of how I got to that border, and how I moved to one or another side of it. This essay is digitally-born in the second decade of the 21st century, so it partakes of the virtual side of the border, but its story and sentiments are from a lost handwritten notebook from 1960, born of the print world which was a partisan of reality for the first half of the 20th century. Either side of the border between the "real" and the "virtual" is a province of a technology: print in the 20th century, digitization in the 21st. The border looks now like a dotted line over the head of a cartoon character, soon to dissolve like clouds in Wordsworth's poem.

*August 7, 2011-February 10, 2012*

---

[135] Everything of consequence takes place at a border. Between the inside and the outside is the skin, the body's largest organ. Most human-made borders in their present form are dissolving, but natural and imaginary frontiers brought about by ends and beginnings have to be recreated to mark the vanished authority and signal the presence of the new. This essay has attempted to articulate personal frontiers at the moment of crossing them: between sexual and political virtualities, between the lost notebook and the registered typewriter, between the East and West of the Cold War, between communist handwriting and American keyboards, between book and screen, between innocence and experience. What is the moment? It's when time's distilled revelation comes up like orgasm, the surprise of intuitive cosmic knowledge. Can it be archived? The Archives is a death mask that preserves only the wisdom or confusion of the *last* moment, when it slips from the surprised face. Moments live and die more often in places brimming with soul: there is where Archives should be located, close to the last expression of the moment, not in secret bunkers. The digitized City on the Hill is Disneyworld.

# ABOUT THE AUTHOR

Andrei Codrescu, pronounced Code-rescue, was born in Sibiu, Romania. His first name "Andrei" comes from the Greek, meaning "man." His last name "Codrescu" is Romanian for "woodsman." He is a man sent by the woods to rescue the (language) code. The trees have named him their liason for the Transition from Book to Screen. For more on the author, see *codrescu.com*.